The 'I Am' Principle

The 'I Am' Principle
The Christ Within

Rev. Fr. Charles Ogada
Edited by Maria Jory

Someone asked Jesus:
"When will the Kingdom of God come?"
And Jesus said to them:
"The Kingdom of God does not admit of observation.
And there will be no one to say 'Look, here it is!' or
'Look, It is over there!' For the Kingdom of God is within you"
Luke 17:20-21

Looking for God is like looking for your own eyes.
You find it when you stop looking. You are that.

BOOKS

Winchester, UK
Washington, USA

First published by O-Books, 2011
O-Books is an imprint of John Hunt Publishing Ltd., The Bothy, Deershot Lodge, Park Lane, Ropley,
Hants, SO24 0BE, UK
office1@o-books.net
www.o-books.com

For distributor details and how to order please visit the 'Ordering' section on our website.

Text copyright: Rev. Fr. Charles Ogada 2010

ISBN: 978-1-84694-540-3

A CIP catalogue record for this book is available from the British Library.

Design: David Kerby

Printed in the UK by CPI Antony Rowe
Printed in the USA by Offset Paperback Mfrs, Inc

We operate a distinctive and ethical publishing philosophy in all
areas of our business, from our global network of authors to
production and worldwide distribution.

To the Spiritans
...Who embody the Spirit

CONTENTS

FOREWORD

There is no question whatsoever, that this is one of the most important books ever written on the subject of the Christian Faith. For the very first time it shines a strong, clear and powerful light on what many Christian's and others intuitively knew, but found difficult to prove, that the Lord Jesus Christ was a veritable Non-Dualist through and through!

Traditionally the Christian Churches have always seen Jesus as the Son of God who came to bring his gospel message, but they never came fully to terms, or followed these non-dual statements through to their ultimate meaning, with his radical utterances such as "The Kingdom of Heaven is Within", "I and My Father are One", and "I am the Way, the Truth and the Light" and so forth. These high pronouncements conform with the mystical non-dual teachings of all the Higher Religions, which teach that God should be known and seen as fully immanent in the heart, rather than as a transcendent Deity out there, as it were; and that there is no division between him and his Father, the Godhead, they are absolutely One! And furthermore that same God is immanent in each immortal soul, and is the Light, the Truth and the Way, the means to find the soul's salvation from its alienation with its own True Nature, the Divine residing within his or her own heart.

It can be readily argued that one of the main causes of Christ's eventual crucifixion was the suspicion by the Sadducees and Pharisees, because of his Non-Dual statements, that he was blaspheming against the orthodox transcendentalism of Judaism, and therefore they did not interfere with the judgement of the Roman Authorities, who believed that he may well be a political threat to the State.

In this wonderful book, and no words are adequate to praise its virtues, Father Charles Ogada proves by chapter and verse the indubitable certainty of Jesus Christ's total Non-Dualism, and gives the many keys to understanding this fact by precise scriptural references, and his own knowledge based on an extensive spiritual enquiry.

Because of his own long grounding, both in traditional Christianity, along with a deep study of the mystical traditions of Hinduism's Advaita Vedanta, Islam's Sufism, and Judaism's Kaballah he is able to point the way to a practical understanding and the full implications of this essential Truth with the utmost clarity.

He succinctly explains all the theological implications and practicalities of the great 'I AM' PRINCIPLE, which was first revealed to Moses, directly by the Godhead speaking from the burning bush in the immortal words, that his Name was 'I AM THAT I AM' and followed through in practice by the Lord Jesus Christ.

The 'I AM' PRINCIPLE is the essential core of the book and hence its title. In its lucid chapters the author graphically explains his own search for truth, his hard struggle with Christian Orthodoxy and his eventual realization that Christ's Non Dual Teachings conform with the other mystical traditions and ways of the Great Higher Religions.

This marvelous book is easy to read because Father Ogada has a fluent command of the English language. All his statements are fully reinforced by scriptural quotation wherever possible.

I am absolutely certain that this book will be a revelation to all devout Christians searching for the deepest and highest meaning of their Faith, and its infallible way to Salvation!

Alan Jacobs
President of the Sri Ramana Maharshi Foundation UK.

EDITOR'S NOTE

Working with Father Charles Ogada, on this book of the "'I am' principle" has been a living experience of the 'Christ' within. The myriad events that occurred in making this book manifest are too many to mention. I am certain, of one thing though, that this 'instrument' called Maria Jory, had no control of any events that unfolded in the part she played in making this book 'happen'. I will never stop being in awe at witnessing the 'divine plan' unfold, how synchronicities come together and how the Divine Puppeteer decides how we mere puppets act out our various roles.

I normally migrate, like the birds, from the English winter, for a five-month sabbatical, to the sunshine of my apartment in Puttaparthi, India and have done so for eighteen years. Puttaparthi is a sacred location where Sri Sathya Sai Baba was born and has his ashram. Spiritual seekers from a variety of nations in the world make pilgrimages to this hallowed township in their thousands.

Father Charles planned to offer a Mass after Christmas in Puttaparthi in December 2009. He needed an organist for the event and a mutual Italian friend recommended me to fill the role. After discussing the music for the Mass, Father Charles and I talked at length. On hearing his story, I made a casual remark to him that he should write down his spiritual experiences. He replied that he was already in the process of writing a book about the Advaitic teachings of Jesus.

The subject of Advaita (non-dualism) has always been very dear to my heart. I had already transcribed, collated and edited a book, some years before, on the Advaitic teachings of the Sage Nisargadatta Maharaj called 'Beyond Freedom' and when I heard about the subject of the book Father Charles was writing, I witnessed myself offering to help edit his book!

Whilst still in India, I began work on editing this book and discussed practicalities over numerous telephone conversations between Father

Charles in Nigeria and me in India. We both realized that the distance separating us was not beneficial in working effectively and I then found myself offering to visit Father Charles in Nigeria!

I returned home to England in spring 2010 and made immediate plans to visit Nigeria. Acquiring a Nigerian visa was quite a challenge with many requirements. The authorities informed me that the visa could take up to ten working days. I had already booked a flight before I had realized I needed a visa and had to change the flight just in case the visa did not arrive on time. Then the volcano erupted in Iceland and all flights in and out of the UK were suspended. I changed my plans yet again.

Finally, I was able to leave for Nigeria. I arrived in Lagos, flew to Port Harcourt and after a long drive arrived in the rural area and parish of St. John at Ebe where Father Charles resides. I awoke every morning to the crow of the resident cockerel and the chanting of the priests in the parish. The peace and quiet of Ebe was conducive to working on the book.

I am from a Catholic background and studied at a convent boarding school. Along the way, I investigated many religions and was even ordained as an Interfaith Minister in 1998. It has been most rewarding working together with Father Charles in 'Satsang.' The profound teachings of Jesus in this book summarized the Advaitic teachings of the various Masters of the different traditions that I had investigated over the years and I returned, full circle, to my Catholic roots.

It has been a privilege to work with Father Charles on such a special book and I have valued each moment of the creative process. My weeks here absorbed in the wisdom of Jesus' teachings, refining each detail and concept during editing, have been a great aid in allowing the teaching to take root and integrate. I feel certain this book will be of great help to readers of all faiths in understanding the real meaning of Jesus' teachings on the 'I am' principle and the 'Christ' within.

Maria Jory
May 2010

ACKNOWLEDGEMENTS

Self Knowledge is that Living Spring which, when you drink it you will never be thirsty again.[1] Many have helped in the process of directing and redirecting this fountain into a reservoir of wisdom which you are holding in your hand. Hence, I am aware I am just a drop in the ocean of the events that happened in the book process. Through the 'I am', I thank everyone whom the 'Christ' has used as instrument in the writing of this book.

To Ted and Jody, in the US, who are the embodiments of love, I owe my deepest gratitude for their loving support and inspiration.

To Karl Meissnitzer, Venkatesh Varan and Denise Breit who painstakingly proof read the original manuscript, my loving appreciation.

To all those who have stood with me in solidarity and love, Hajia Funmi Bodunde, Justice (Mrs) Chinwe Emembolu, Chief Okezie Nwabuko, Mrs Uzoma Udoye, Dr. Jayaram Barathi, Dr. Anupata Roy, Mr. Harish Chulani, Kelechi Emeagi, Nooshin Mehrabani, Bishu Prusty, Mark Aspa, Ebele Ibada, Joy Arazu, and Adaeze Iloeje; the Families of Prof. (Mrs.) Adiele Nwosu, Prof. I. C. Iloeje, Mrs. Mba Angela, Mr. Felix Onwudinjo, Mr. Tony Tabansi, Victor and Genoviva Kanu in Zambia, Denise Breit and Rich Bombace, Ron and Su Farmer of Australia, Karl and Catherine Meissnitzer in Austria, and Raguvir Kaur of Singapore, I am eternally grateful.

I am indebted to my parents, Bernard and Bibianna, who made so much spiritual impact in my early life, to my brothers and sisters, Chinyere, Chika, Ngozi, Ugonna, Udoka, Chidimma, Kelechi and Jane, who have been a great source of love and inspiration, and to my grandmother, Mrs Paulina Agu, who is always fond of me.

My thanks go to Maria Jory, the 'lion' of truth. Through the creative process, of deleting repetitions, correcting the tenses, refining the sentences, clarifying the concepts, removing ambiguities, you made the book shine like a crystal. It has been a joy working with you especially when you played the devil's advocate! More than mere editing, your deep knowledge of the subject of non-dualism was invaluable.

I wish to acknowledge the role of the Spiritans who have nurtured the Spirit within me, my teachers in the Seminary who gave me the tools for critical enquiry, my fellow priests, especially Fr. Dom Nnoshiri, who gave me the sacred space I most needed in the parish to complete this book.

To the Catholic Church, the very embodiment of the 'Christ' principle, this book could not have been born without you.

To the spiritual masters, Sri Ramana Maharshi, St John of the Cross, and Anthony de Mello, who were 'pointers' to the pathless path of the 'I'-less 'I am', I offer my humble salutations!

To Bhagavan Sri Sathya Sai Baba, who brought me 'face to face' with the 'Christ' within, and made me stand without a stand, I am that I am.[2]

15th May, 2010

INTRODUCTION

From childhood, I had the habit of withdrawing into the thick of the African jungle. The trees talked to me. Their language filled my heart with inexplicable peace and joy. During one of those solitary moments, I had an unusual experience. I was 17 years old at the time.

I was alone with the trees, filled with the stillness of an unknown presence. Suddenly a strange force took over me. My heart started expanding as if my body was getting bigger and bigger. Then I heard a voice. This voice filled my heart with so much love. I dissolved in it. The sound of the voice was directionless. I lost all sense of separation from the things around me - as if the trees, the soil, the sky, were part of my body.

The voice said to me, "What would you want to do with this life?", and I replied, "What else Father but to give this life to you." I use the word 'replied' because there is no other word to describe my experience, as I did not feel any difference between the voice and myself. I was aware that this voice was the living sound that kept everything in being, yet I was one with it.

The sweetness of this voice became my food, my sleep, my dream, my thought, my breath, and my all. It was a living awareness, which made me feel the pain or joy in everything because I felt them in my heart. Everything was like one continuum of life-streaming energy. In a moment, I knew there was nothing apart from the Spirit.

The impact of this experience remained with me for about two weeks. Then I started thinking about a way to give this life to the Father[1]. Prior to this encounter, I was preparing to study medicine in the university. I had just finished high school and was waiting for my results. Then, I changed my mind because I felt that the best way to actualize my mystical experience was by joining a religious order. I then sought to become a member of the congregation of the Holy Ghost Fathers and Brothers, known as the Spiritans. In 1703, in France, Venerable Father Claude Pourlat de Place founded this international missionary order of men who committed their lives for the service of the poor.

I joined this order the following year, 1989, as a seminarian studying to become a Catholic priest. Initially everything was beautiful. God filled me with so much spiritual favor and sweetness. However, along the way, the bliss of my mystical experience began to recede.

During the ninth year of my studies to the priesthood, my world finally collapsed. The emptiness that enveloped me was darker than death. I could no longer find the One who was the light of my being. Life was dead and dry. The little flicker of the Divine radiance that kept my soul going had finally blown out, and everything was hidden from me. Completely lost in the void of meaninglessness, my soul wandered in the darkness of existence. The will to live was gone. Like a body severed from its life breath, my soul pined in vain for the eternal source of its being. I reached the end of my strength and decided to leave the Seminary, as I could no longer withstand the test. I knew that this decision was not going to solve my problem but I also knew that I could no longer endure the burden of the darkness.

During this time, my beloved Dad got very sick and sent word that I should come home immediately. I went home to see him. He was fifty-eight years old then and was dying of cancer. The pains were excruciating. He could not stand, sit or lie down. Every posture he took brought him pangs of agony, and in his pains, I forgot my pains. His darkness swallowed my darkness. I was like someone who forgot his mild headache because of a severe toothache. My journey with him in his suffering and death became a new awakening for me, a strong push that pulled me to seek the deeper realities of life. My Dad's encounter led me to the limits of the human mind and I discovered that beyond the logic of reason, suffering pulls us to that void of surrender where we are untouched by suffering.

My father passed through this transformative power of suffering.

Initially he rejected the sickness asking, "Why me Lord?" Then gradually, this rejection gave way to acceptance and acceptance led to surrender. Once he called me to his bedside and said he was on his way to Calvary. Calvary is the Christian symbol of complete surrender or the dissolution of the ego on the cross. He asked me to request Novena masses (nine days' Christian religious prayer) be said for him asking for God's strength and courage to reach Calvary. Then he said to me, "I am offering these sufferings for the joy of the world, for the souls in purgatory and for the happiness of the family".

Towards the end, our Dad's attitude of surrender in suffering brought him in contact with his inner Self. In that mystical union, although there was pain, there was no suffering. It was as if he had discovered the secret of death. There was light and joy in his eyes and the constant chanting of the sweetness of God's names anointed his lips. It was unusual and very rare for one to know the hour of one's death, yet three days before his death, he called us to his bedside (my mother, my immediate younger brother and myself) and told us he would leave his body the following Wednesday. This was on Monday, 25 August 1997. He told us to be ready and prepare for what was going to happen on that day. Of course, we did not take him seriously because we did not want to believe that he was leaving us. On that Wednesday, about 3:45 pm, he called the three of us again by his bedside and said, 'It is time.' He gave me his hand and instructed me to chant the names of God. We started reciting the litany of the sacred 'Names of Jesus.' It was while we were chanting these holy names of God that he left his body like one who had fallen asleep.

The suffering and death of my Dad was a hard push that pulled me inwards and reawakened the dying embers of my spiritual quest. His words at his deathbed became the bedrock on which my spirit soared again to the mysteries of Silence. He told me not to leave the seminary, so I returned in obedience to his command and to the joy of this newfound energy, which held the prospect of connecting me back to my ancient roots.

"And our souls were roused up...
From the depths of Silence
Like the rising of a star
From the void of space
Its light could no longer be hidden
in the dark of the night sky
A Crisis in the Seminary
The birth of a great Spiritual awakening"

The Spiritan International School of Theology (SIST) was where I received my final training in the priesthood. Students from different African countries and cultural backgrounds created a unique environment of cross-fertilization of ideas and a deep respect and openness to different perspectives of Truth. It was a community of unity where every member was a Spiritan, meaning Embodiment of Spirit. We strived to live the life of inner spiritual transformation according to the calling of our religious vocation.

The theological training was the final stage in the long ten to eleven years of formation before the Seminarian was finally ordained a priest. At the midstream of this last stage of formation, which spanned a period of four years, we were required to make a final commitment to the three evangelical vows of Poverty, Chastity and Obedience. Our lives as a community of brothers revolved around these vows. This final commitment, usually made at the eighth year of training, was the greatest event in the life of the community. It was a radical calling to the Spiritans to be and to live as Christ in total detachment from material things and the sense of 'me' and 'mine' (the vow of Poverty); a life of purity and mystical union with God (the vow of Chastity) and in complete surrender to the Will of the Father (the vow of Obedience). It was a call to a Divine Life and the sole goal of the training of a Spiritan according to our Spiritan Rule of Life (SR) was to awaken this Christ Consciousness within the hearts of the students.[2]

One could not aspire to anything greater in life. However, after making my final commitment to this sublime life of holiness, I knew there was something still missing within me. I could not find God. I felt disconnected from the voice that called me. My heart was dry. I saw the same spiritual aridity all around me and I used to wonder whether it was a projection of my inner state. Was I the only one involved in this play of pretence, my spirit wondered. I did not want to be untrue to myself. Yet when our Dad had told me to return to the seminary, I knew I would one day find the source of my being. "How could I connect to that Source?" This dilemma entrapped my soul. "Who could show me the way?" was the unspoken anguish of my heart.

Then something happened. It was the root of a crisis, which engulfed the Seminary. There came from the Governing Board of the Spiritan International School of Theology, a decree addressed to the students through the Directors of formation. The letter and its mandate gave students the opportunity to give a feedback on the manner in which they were being trained. The students saw this opportunity as the "Moment of Divine grace".[3] Since this mandate was coming from the highest authority of the institute, the students decided to empty unto the bosom of the Supreme Mother, the burden in their hearts, the anguish of their frustrated hopes, the tension of their stressed emotions and most importantly, the aridity of their spiritual aspirations. The students spoke with one heart and one soul for a radical transformation in the process of their formation.

I did not realize until then that the inner spiritual yearnings of my heart were the unspoken desires of many students. My frustrations were their suppressions and my spiritual deadlock, their very inner experience although in varying degrees. They stood up to the challenge of the moment with an unparalleled momentum.

To harmonize their ideas the students set up a committee made up of seven students and I was elected to be one of the members of this body. This committee worked tirelessly every day and into the late hours of the night. They had to harmonize the ideas and deliberations of the students into a systematic and coherent whole. There were general meetings of the entire student-body, where fundamental issues, pertaining to the integral aspects of their formation, were discussed and deliberated. At the end of each general meeting, the special committee would retire back to work in order to come up with a simple summary that would give a precise representation of the expressions of the students. At the end, this summary was presented, once again, to the general student-body for corrections, amendments and final approval. Each integral aspect of formation passed through this purifying process. At the end, the students came up with a document entitled "The Students' Preparatory Paper for the Spiritan Community Customary Review" which came to be known as the "Moment of Grace" document.

When the appointed time came, the SIST governing Council sent a delegate to represent the Council in the deliberations that would take place between the Directors of formation, the Rector of the Seminary and student representatives. The students had elected two seats in this committee and I was one of them. During the course of the deliberations, we presented to the committee, the students' preparatory paper. It took the committee a whole day to digest the contents of this document that was an opus magnum in every respect.

The students' review of the community customary, henceforth called the "Moment of Grace" document, was influenced by five major principles.

First is the need to bridge the gap between the spiritual truths encoded in our Spiritan Rule of Life and its concrete realization in the inner Rule of the Spiritan lived experience. According to the students, "Our experience as 'Spiritans' in the initial formation is that of nostalgia: we yearn with unfulfilled hope when we will live our professed religious vocation."[4] Hence, the "Moment of Grace" document laid bare the existential questions encountered by the students in their effort to live according to the three apostolic vows of Celibacy, Poverty and Obedience, which formed the very core of our religious vocation.

How could we cope with the solitude of the celibate life without that mystical experience where the male and the female principles became one and the inside became the outside in the ecstasy of Divine union?

How could we cope with the ancient awakening of the serpent hood coiled at the waist, without the flute of the celestial music that swallowed its poison?

How could one strip oneself of the poverty clothing of 'me' and 'mine' without that Divine fire of wisdom that burned the seed of desire?

How could one relinquish the imperative of self-will on the cross of total self-surrender to the Divine Omni will without access to that ancient key that opens the 'Void of Silence' wherein there was no second?

Although the system in which we found ourselves held in its vision the great spiritual ideals of Divine Life, it could not offer us practical steps that could unify the transcendental heights of idealism with the immanent world of pragmatism.[5]

The "Moment of Grace" document further stressed the need for a Master–disciple relationship paradigm of formation; an example where Formation took the form of the transformation found in a workshop with practical tools of 'hammers' and 'nails', 'chisels' and 'brushes'; a Formation where the Master-apprentice relationship gave primacy to the authority of experience.[6] But where could we find such a Master, whose thought, word and deed was unified and whose Presence was the Silence that transformed the Spirit? This was the anguished cry of the Seminarians to her Mother in the heavenly dome of Rome.

Theology complicates one's understanding of God. It piles God away in the library of books. It burdens our heads with images, pictures, and ideas about God and leaves our hearts dry with longing. We were tired of seeing pictures of God. We were weary of reading about God. We wanted to experience God.

There had to be a synthesis between love and discipline. Love could be killed with the rod of discipline. Yes, the Holy Book said, "Spare the rod and spoil the child"[7] but it never said, "Kill the child with the rod". A child without love was as good as dead. Thus, the document was of the opinion that the hand that disciplined had to be in synthetic harmony with the heart that loves. Otherwise, discipline became an empty and momentary exercise. This was the situation in the seminary. Most of the students just obeyed the rules but never believed in them. They obeyed the rules to escape the punishment imposed by its breakage. They adhered to the laws for the sole goal of becoming a priest. Once this objective was secure, all rules were then thrown to the winds. The "Moment of Grace" document emphasized a training that made students masters of the law instead of slaves of the law where they always wanted to get out of the yoke of the law through ordination. To be a Master of the law was to realize that zenith where all laws merge into one – the law of love. That law was the immortal knowledge of the Self – that knowledge, which was the Truth that set people free from the very bondage of the law.[8]

The "Moment of Grace" document acknowledged that the discipline of love would take time, beyond the rod of discipline that lasted as long as the rod was in the hand; the discipline of love was eternal, transcending the barriers of space and the limitations of time, because its source is from within. And to tap that source required patience; that power which helped us to live in the present; that energy which actualized the full potential of the moment because it converged our energy at a point – the Now – without the worries of the future and its results and without the regrets of the past and its burdens. With patience, the discipline of love can transform the students and make their actions emanate from the Truth of their inner conviction, that sacred sound of God resounding clearly in the sanctum of their hearts.

On the other hand, the rod of discipline expected and got quick results. It made seminarians 'Saints' overnight by multiplying laws and laying it on them as a yoke of burden. The rod of discipline turned students into hypocrites, always acting and reacting because of external stimuli and when the rod was out of sight, the 'sinner' in the Seminarian showed its ugly face.

Finally and most importantly, the "Moment of Grace" document was a prayer for Divine intervention. It prayed for Divine grace in the spiritual predicament of the students because it acknowledged that the "work of holiness itself was the very action of the Holy Ghost." The document did not lay blame on the Formators because they were also products of the same system. Rather, the document was a genuine and sincere expression of the existential situation in which the students found themselves. We knew this chasm. We felt it in the marrow of our bones. Sometimes we had to follow the tide of the mundane, and when the tension got too tight, a student would crack a joke to the humor of those who pulled long faces: "Are you the one who killed Jesus?" Why worry about things you cannot change?

The Seminarians were good mannered and the Priests who were training them were great souls of immeasurable value. All who had joined the sacred brotherhood had made a fundamental option in life: to follow Jesus in the totality of His personality. This fundamental option gave them a disposition to what was good, beautiful and true.

However, somewhere along the line, the system had lost that 'Tree of Life' that connected it to the ancient streams of holiness. We had lost the Jesus Tradition in the pile of orthodoxy. We had lost the ancient key to the sanctuary of 'One', the 'Sanctum Sanctorum', because we had not paid heed to the secret teachings that Jesus gave to his disciples in private.[9] We were engrossed with the objective and had lost the subjective. Yet we knew that the Truth was in the subjective. All things of which we were aware were but manifestations of a 'Reality' of which we were unaware. We labelled this hidden tradition as occult and filed them away as non-canonical. Then we turned around to build structures and superstructures that had no substructure. We had forgotten that the Jesus Secret traditions were hidden from the learned and the wise and revealed only to simple children.[10] The scholars were not able to understand them from books as they were beyond the descriptions of letters and alphabets. They transcended the explanations of words and language.

The "Moment of Grace" document was a shock to our Formators. Its awakening power imposed the challenges of change in the new dynamic approach to formation. It received the full support of the SIST Governing Council who in turn placed this challenge on the team of Formation at home. However, one fundamental issue loomed in the minds of our Formators. It was like the dilemma of the mother who knew the medicine that could cure the disease of the child, but who was unaware how to procure the elixir. We all knew the truth embodied in our Spiritan Rule of Life, but how were we to actualize the Truth that set people free from the disease of death and ignorance was the problem that eluded our wits.

This created panic and real anxiety in the hearts of our Formators. Their questions arose from a genuine concern born from human experience. "How could one dismantle the tattered thatch that gave shade to the homeless on a utopia that promised a city of mansions?" "How could one let go of the single bird in the hand in search of an unknown two in the forest?" "How could one let the students have the freedom they were seeking without the guarantee of that inner responsibility that made them free?"

They were right. They foresaw a crisis within the walls of the seminary. They felt the looming revolution that could either bring about a total dissolution to the labors of the past or the rebirth of a new life. Initially, for about two weeks, the students and Formators were working in the bond of the brotherhood, with renewed enthusiasm, day and night, in conferences and workshops, in groups and sub groups, to come up with a common standard that would bring about the realization of the concerns of the document. We all felt the hand of the Holy Spirit leading us to the heights of our dream.

Then something happened. Time stopped at the top of the pick. Everything tumbled down. One fateful afternoon, I received a letter from the Director of Formation. When I opened it, my heart dropped. It read that I and another student that wrote the document were to be no longer in the Seminary with immediate effect. We had to leave the walls of the Seminary within three hours from the time we received our letters of expulsion and we were never to come back or be admitted to any community of fellowship. My soul broke down in lamentation:

Oh, Beloved Mother!
For nine years, you nurtured me
In the comforts of your womb
And fed me with the milk from your bosom
For nine years, you gave me shelter
At the pillars of your altar

With the strength of a mighty eagle
You protected me
And with the garments of salvation
You clothed me

Now you throw me away
When I was due to be born
Doomed to live in exile
Who can now give me the elixir?

I left the confines of the Seminary that evening, the 3rd of March 1998. I did not know where to go. I had no other home that I could call mine and no place, where I could lay my head. I could not carry this burden to my mother as she was just recovering from the loss of her dear husband.

My mind was blank
My legs were heavy
With no direction and without a destination
I stood in the middle of nowhere
Not knowing where to turn

Then Jesus turned!
And He was by my side
Above, below, around, within,
"Why fear", He said, "when I am now here"

With his love in my heart, I went into inner solitude, for hours and hours at a stretch, he immersed me in the bliss of his love. Oblivious of the world around me, my beloved took me to the inner world of the Spirit. He fed me with Divine strength and my body so fragile required little or no physical food.

Back in the Seminary, life stood still. The centre could not hold again. Like the phantom of the graveyard, the "Moment of Grace" document was buried in the tomb of silence and students moved about in hushed whispers dumbfounded at the twist of events. The anguished expressions on their silent faces were too dense to put into words: "If you expelled them, you have to expel us too. For we all wrote the document. We all signed it with the seal of our blood and wrote it with the very drops of our lives."

An impenetrable stillness descended on the Seminary. When they gathered for spiritual communion, there was a deep silence, interrupted occasionally by the sobs of a broken heart. When they assembled for meals, there was no appetite for food and when it was time for recreation, they walked about in silence since life had lost its zest.

Then something happened. This was the last beat that broke the dance of the spirits. It was evident that the seminary was heading for a collapse if nothing urgent and drastic happened to salvage the situation. An idea arose in the congregation of the priests to expel any student who did not comply to the old order starting with the deacons. (The deacons were the most senior group of the seminarians and some of the deacons were members of the committee that wrote the "Moment of Grace" document. Before our expulsion, we were 17 deacons in all.)

When this decision was made, the remaining deacons were summoned individually, before a panel of the fathers. Standing in the middle and surrounded by the authority that held the vocation, each one of the deacons were given the 'Bull of Expulsion'. He had an interval of five minutes to carefully digest and ingest its content after which he was required to either sign or not to sign, to be or not to be. To sign the Bull meant that one agreed to disassociate oneself totally from anything pertaining to the "Moment of Grace" document and hence forth to abide totally with the old rules of the Seminary. Not to sign meant an immediate expulsion from the Seminary.

One could not possibly begin to understand the implications and the burden of decision in which each of the deacons had to make within an interval of five minutes when one took into consideration the religious, social, economical and cultural impacts on the Seminarian. Here was the deacon who had spent seventeen solid years of his life and youth (if we were to include the six years of training in the junior seminary) for a vision which was about to be ruptured. A mere signature would dissolve a whole life vision and dream! Eight deacons signed the document. Seven did not sign. These seven had to leave the Seminary that same day. Later on, more students, including the rest of the seven members of the committee who produced the "Moment of Grace" document had to leave. At last, there was sanity in the seminary.

The 'Mother House' in Rome came to know about the crisis that had engulfed the seminary because of the "Moment of Grace" document. Many students had cried to the Mother in Rome for her intervention – "Do you not care if we perish?" [11] When I learnt about the predicament of the other students, I was also compelled to write to Rome an epistle of love beckoning her to save her children. That letter, which was close to 40 typed pages, was written not because of any desire to be called back to the seminary but for the sake of the students who were suffering on account of their inner quest for Truth.

After sending my letter to Rome, I went into a desert prayer to recollect myself for a new way of life at the Benedictine Monastery, Ewu, in Edo State. This was about 800 kilometres away from the Seminary. I was secretly happy that I could now seek the Truth beyond the boundaries of the church. In fact, my Spirit was calling me to the East. I had read so much about the Eastern masters and my heart held the prospect that they could have the practical elixir to the human quest.

While I was in the Monastery one afternoon, I had an urgent call from my seminary. The message was that our Superior General (the highest authority in our order) had come from Rome to our Seminary and wanted to see me immediately. My spirit was torn, I was happy that the Mother had come to save her children. I was also sad that this might mean a delay in my journey to the East. However, because of compassion for the Seminarians, I left the Monastery the morning of the following day and arrived at the Seminary in the evening.

When I arrived, the Superior General called me to a private audience and we sat, like mother and child, and talked for close to one hour. He had a deep understanding of the anguish of the Seminarians, their yearning for spiritual intimacy and the poverty of the mother to satisfy their spiritual hunger. He said that the 'Mother House' was deeply concerned about the issues raised in our individual letters to Rome and in the "Moment of Grace" document.

With his loving persuasions, all the brothers who had been asked to leave the seminary were recalled. His love was overwhelming. He initiated a process of reconciliation and healing in the Seminary. He sat in patience, for hours at a stretch, having a personal audience with each priest and each of the Formators and with many of the students who needed the healing touch of his presence. After the personal interviews, he called and spoke to us in groups and sub groups creating and broadening the solidarity of fellowship. He brought joy and hopes into our hearts and revived our dropping spirits.

He spoke to us every morning as we gathered at the table of our Heavenly Father and shared the sacred Bread of Life, the Holy Communion of the eternal Presence. He sat with us every evening at the table of our earthly mother as we partook from the bountiful sumptuousness of her riches, the Tree of Life. He stayed with us for close to two weeks. When he left, his presence lingered on, in our hearts.

He gave his holy instructions that all the deacons who had been sent away be raised to the sacred order of the eternal priesthood that same year (six out of the eight deacons who had signed the document had already been ordained priests). While we were away, the final examination for our Masters Degree in Theology took place. In his heart so broad, he also arranged that those of us who had missed this examination be given the opportunity to write it. The Duquesne University, Pittsburgh, USA was to set this fresh examination. Such was the extent of the love that we experienced from the Mother General in Rome.

Thus, on the 4th of December 1999, one of the Bishops in the fellowship ordained the eleven brothers priests in the Catholic order of Melchizedek, and that was how I became a priest.

Moreover, the prophecy was fulfilled when at two I told my father, 'I am your Father'. In addition, from then on, they called me 'Nna'[12] which means 'Father' for the 'Father' (Yahweh or I am) is in all of us and we are one with the 'Father'.[13]

After my ordination, the seeker within me woke up. Who is Jesus? Who am I? These were the basic questions of my life. My ten long years of studies in the seminary could not answer them. Although I talked and preached about Jesus, I realized I did not know him. I had not yet unraveled the mystery of the Christ. Nevertheless, even more frustrating was the fact that I knew I did not know myself. My own reality was a more frustrating mystery. If I did not know myself, how could I hope to know God? I was determined to resolve these two mysteries. It was as if this was the very purpose for my birth.

Before ordination, each Spiritan was allowed to choose where he wanted to work during the duration of his first appointment. I had chosen to study Eastern Religion hoping this would give me the opportunity to get a posting in the land of the East, which was legendary in revealing the secrets of the Masters. Nevertheless, Divinity had different plans, and I received a posting, instead, to work in my native country as an associate pastor in the Archdiocese of Lagos.

Although my body was at home, my spirit was in India. I applied for my annual leave that same year and I hastened to India like a deer yearning for running streams. In that sacred land, I met with Masters who had realized the essence of the Spirit. Blessed was the one who found a Living Master. A journey of a thousand years took only a few days.

I met Sri Sathya Sai Baba, an Indian Holy man in 2001. Through him, I discovered that the Christ I sought in books and lectures, in churches and pilgrimages, through valleys and hills, across seas and oceans, and amidst tears and joys, was actually closer to me than my very breath. From 'interviews' (dualism) he led me to 'inner views' (Qualified Non-dualism), and from 'inner views', to 'no-view' (Advaita or non-dualism). It was a sigh of relief when I found that the one seeking was the One Sought! The very worshiper was the One Worshiped. The knower was the one known. The Christ was not different from who I was in essence.

The following year, I visited India again. By the time, I returned to the parish where I was working in Nigeria, things had fallen apart. My visit to India was held in great suspicion by the church authorities and I was temporarily dismissed from my priestly duties. Suddenly, I had no job, no home, and no socially-defined identity. This was the unfolding of the divine plan. Stripped of all my identifications, I was free to be!

I visited India, sometimes twice every year for ten years and stayed as long as my permit allowed. At the abode of Prashanthi Nilayam in Puttaparthi and in the cave of the sacred Mountain of Arunachala, in Tiruvanamalai, my spirit began to unfold its wondrous mysteries. I realized that the mystery of Christ was hidden within the mystery of my Self.

This book represents the essence of my twenty years of spiritual search as far as it can be conveyed in words. It has been written in a question and answer format. The questions represent the doubts with which I had battled over the years. The answers came like ripples of bliss during deep states of awareness of the Christ within. Common names in the Bible, especially those of the disciples, have been used to express the questions. Every spiritual seeker is a disciple. The Self, which Christians refer to as the 'Christ' is the Master. When the seeker becomes aware of the Self, all doubts disappear.

The 'I am' principle is the true meaning of Christianity. It is the 'Christ' within. It is the mystery of the 'Self' unraveled, which means, 'the Self alone exists'. Everything is Spirit. You are that which you are looking for. You are the one who has multiplied itself as the many. The book you are reading is the mystery teachings of Jesus on the 'Self' and one of the infinite ways to the pathless One.

The 'I am' principle is also the essence of all religions. Vedanta is at the heart of Hinduism.[14] The Sufi teachings are at the core of Islam.[15] Kabala is the fundamental expression of Judaism. Zen is the real meaning of Buddhism. These essences represent a point where all religions become one, and where all distinctions of creeds, dogmas, and rituals disappear. For those who have realized the one, there are no religious differences. The 'I am' principle is inherent in all the above traditions and is the essence of the teachings of Jesus.

This book holds the key to the power of the 'I am' within you. Do not read with your head if you want to tap into your inner source.

Rather, allow your heart to dance in the music of its notes. The reason is that the Self can only be experienced but not explained. The goal of every word and concept in this book is to take you to an inner experiential awareness. Immediately you experience, you will know that words are only signposts to the Self.

If this Book gets into your hands, it means you are ready to receive it. Leave the things you are unable to understand. The Self is the Source. The more you force, the more you move away from your Self. Christ is your Self. Christ is within you. This book will have achieved its mission if it takes you to your Christ-Source, which is the Self.

At the end of your spiritual quest, you must do away with this book and indeed with every book! This is because you cannot find the Self in books. When a thorn pricks your foot, you use another thorn to remove it and after that, both thorns are unnecessary. Ideas, concepts, imaginations and other mental stuff are the last obstacle towards the experience of the inner Christ. The ideas in your head are the first thorn. The ideas in this book are the second thorn. When the second thorn removes the first, remember to throw both thorns away!

Part I:
The Christ

Peter said to Jesus:
"You are the Christ."
Matthew 16:16

"The Christ is the 'I am' principle."

1
The 'I AM' Principle
...The 'Christ' Within

Jesus said to them:
"The Kingdom of God is within you."
Luke 17:21

When Jesus came in the region of Caesarea Philippi he put this question to his disciples, "Who do people say I am?"[1]
Andrew: Some say you are Elijah or one of the ancient prophets who has come back to life.
But you, who do you say, 'I am'?
Peter: You are the Christ.
You are blessed, Simon son of Jonah! Your statement is the foundation of faith and the key to the Kingdom of God within you. However, you must keep this knowledge to yourselves since the people are not yet ready for it.
Mathew: Beloved Lord, what is the nature of the 'Christ'?
The 'Christ' is the 'I am' Principle. This 'I am' is God. 'I am' God. You too are God.[2] Whenever you say 'I am', know that 'I am' as God. In the Scriptures, when Moses inquired into the nature of God, he realized it as the 'I am'.[3] 'I am that I am' sums up the whole truth.
Thomas: Lord, you are the 'Christ' the only begotten son. Could there be another 'Christ' outside the one 'Christ'?
The Christ is within all. The 'Christ' is your 'I am' and the 'I am' in everything.
Thomas: What then is the difference between your 'I am' and my 'I am' since I cannot do the things you do?
The difference is Awareness. I know that 'I am that I am'. You lack this awareness. I know that 'I am' the Christ. You are ignorant of your Reality. The moment you know yourself, you will do the same things that I do.[4]

Philip: But what exactly is this 'I am'? No one can see the 'I am' or touch it. The 'I am' is Spirit. That is why you cannot see or touch it. It is beyond the grasp of the senses. It is the Divine spark within you and the heart of everything. It is what you call the 'Self', 'Spirit', 'God', 'Christ', 'Consciousness' or any name you may choose to call it. In essence, it is nameless.
John: Lord, how do I know this Christ?

You are looking for Christ where you cannot find it, namely, outside yourself. Christ is the 'I am' in you but you fail to realize this. You are God but you are looking for God. A little story will make this clear to you.

Once upon a time, ten men were on a journey in search of a hidden treasure.[5] On the way, they encountered many troubles but they were able to overcome each one of them because they were united. Finally, they reached a place where they had to cross a river that was flooded.

After swimming across the river and reaching the other shore, they wanted to make sure they had all, in fact, safely crossed the flood. Therefore, they decided to count themselves. One of the ten began to count, but while counting others left himself out. "I see only nine; sure enough we have lost one. Who could it be?" he said. "Did you count correctly?" asked another, and did the counting himself. However, he too counted only nine. One after the other each of the ten counted only nine missing himself. 'We are only nine,' they all agreed, "but who is the missing one?" they asked themselves. Every effort they made to discover the 'missing' individual failed. "Whoever may he be, he is drowned," said the sentimental of the ten fools, "we have lost him". So saying he burst into tears, and the rest of the nine, followed suit.

A sympathetic wayfarer saw them weeping on the riverbank and enquired for the cause of their sorrow. They related what had happened and said that even after counting themselves several times they could find no more than nine. On hearing the story, but seeing all the ten before him, the wayfarer guessed what had happened. In order to make them know for themselves that they were really ten, that all of them had arrived safely from the crossing, he told them, "Let each of you count for himself but one after the other serially, one, two, three and so on. Then I shall give you each a blow so that all of you may be sure of having been included in the count and included only once. The tenth 'missing' man will then be found." Hearing this they rejoiced at the prospect of finding their 'lost' comrade and accepted the method suggested by the wayfarer. While the kind wayfarer gave a blow to each of the ten in turn, he that got the blow counted himself aloud. "Ten" said the last man as he got the last blow in his turn. Bewildered they looked at one another, "We are ten" they said with one voice and thanked the wayfarer for having removed their grief.

This is a parable of how you look for yourself outside yourself. It is the root of all your grief. You think God is missing because you have failed to see Him as your Self. In addition, the more you look for yourself, the more you separate yourself from yourself in self-ignorance. Count your 'Self', first. That is to say, seek first the Kingdom of God.[6] It is within you. It is you. It is everything.

Peter: How do I know myself if I am the one that I am looking for?

Stop looking. Be Still. The moment you stop looking you will discover that you are the one who has reflected itself as the many. What you see is only a reflection of what you are. Everything is a reflection of the Self. Like a dog puzzled by its own image on the mirror, you are mystified by creation which is nothing but the reflection of the 'I am'.[7] The dog takes its own image as another dog and begins to bark at it. As long as the dog fails to understand that there is no 'second' apart from it, (that what it sees is only his own reflection) it will continue to be afraid of its own shadow.

God is your Self. God is your 'I am'. When you look for God, you are bound to see shadows. Hence, all that is required to find God is to be still. The verse, 'Be still and know that I am God'[8] is the essence of all the scriptures put together. It is the negative way. You find God only when you cease looking. You know God only when you go beyond knowledge. You are God only when you die to this false idea that you are not God.[9]

Matthew: Lord, the scriptures tell us that our first parents, Adam and Eve had to leave the Garden of Eden because they wanted to be like God.[10] Why did they have to leave, if they were truly God?

Adam and Eve wanted to be like God. What is the need to want to be that which you already are? This 'wanting' is the problem. It is the origin of desire.[11] Desire is the delusion that makes you think you are separate from the object of your desire. However, since you are everything which you desire, namely the Self, desire makes you look for that which is always with you. You believe God is everywhere, within you, above you, below you, and around you; however, you go on searching for him. If God is omnipresent, how can there be a presence outside God? And if every presence is God's presence, how can you be separated from God? Adam and Eve were never separate from the garden of the 'I am' consciousness.[12] Desire made them think so.

The Adam and Eve principle is in everyone. Adam and Eve, the snake and the forbidden fruit, are allegories referring to the human person. Adam represents the ego. Eve is the mind. The snake symbolizes the senses. The fruit represents the world or the object of sensory perception. Without the ego (Adam) there is no mind (Eve)[13] and without the mind (Eve) there is no objectification (desire for the forbidden fruit).

When the mind (Eve) is turned inwards, the ego (Adam) finds rest in the 'Self' that is God. When, on the other hand, the mind (Eve) turns outwards towards the objects of sensory perception, the ego (Adam) feels 'separated' from the Garden of the Self. Hence, the mind (Eve) is the cause of Adam's bondage or liberation.[14]

James: How does one live without desire?

Know that there was never a time when you were not that which you want to be. Desire is like the mirage in the desert which a man takes to be water until he comes to it and finds it does not exist. Hence, the transcendence of desire is attained not by the fulfillment of desire but by understanding the nature of desire.

James: So is it desire that separates us from God?

The idea of separation is not real but a mental delusion because you cannot be separate even though you may think you are. Divinity is your identity and nothing can change this.

Andrew: Lord, my problem is how to find God. My soul yearns for Him like fish drawn out of water!

Once there was a little fish, which lived in the mighty ocean. This fish was apparently disturbed. All her life she had been seeking to see the ocean. She had traveled everywhere in this search. She had read volumes and volumes of literature about this thing called 'Ocean'. She had also consulted many learned experts on this subject but no one could solve her dilemma. Finally, one day, she came to the whale and posed the question to the whale. She said, "Please brother whale hasten to the prayers of my heart. My soul is yearning for the Ocean. All my life I have heard about this mystery called 'Ocean'. So many people have preached about it and written about it. However, I want to see it, touch it and feel it myself. Please could you show me where I could find this 'Ocean'?"

The big whale laughed to himself and said to the little fish, "Sister fish, look! The reality, which you are touching, swimming in, living in, 'is' the Ocean. It is above you, below you, around you, within you, all over you. In fact, you cannot live a minute without it. It is your very life principle." The little fish could not believe the whale. She said, "What is touching me is water, ordinary water. I want to see the ocean". She went away sad.

You are like the little fish in the Ocean looking for the Ocean. You are in God, above God, below God, around God, within God, as your very existence. Yet you are all the time looking for God. A man looking for God is like someone searching for his own eyes ('I'). Not only are they always with him, but also without them he cannot see what he is looking for. Moreover, since the eyes cannot see itself except in a mirror, when perhaps the man sees his eyes in the mirror of his own reflection; he feels he had found his eyes. However, he did not find his eyes. He brought them with him. The moment you know this Truth, that you are what you are looking for, you will remain still.

Thomas: Lord, you told us to ask and it shall be given, to search and we shall find, to knock and the door shall be opened.[15] *How can we search if we are what we are searching for?*

Seek the Seeker. Find out the one who is searching. Knock at the door of the Self. When you find out the reality of the questioner, namely the 'I am', then you will realize that the knowledge of the 'I am' is the solution to every question that has ever been or will ever be asked. The answer to every human quest is Self knowledge.

On the day you realize that God is not separate from you, at that moment you will know the essence of everything because the 'I am' is the heart of all that is. Without this fundamental knowledge, it is a waste of time trying to grasp the reality of God. When you understand that you are one with God, it becomes very easy to understand every other thing. When you miss this point, nothing else can hold together. In truth, it will be an exercise in futility when you seek to know God as a reality outside yourself. You can only know God on the day you know your Self and you can only know your Self the moment you remain still.

Self Knowledge is that Living Spring which, when you drink it you will never be thirsty again.[16]

2
Self Knowledge
...is the Kingdom of God

God said to Moses:
"I am that I am"...
"This will be my name forever; it has always been my name, and it will be used throughout all generations."
Exodus 3:14-15

Jesus said to his disciples, 'I am' the Way. 'I am' the Truth and the Life. No one can know the Father except through the 'I am'. [1]
Philip: Lord, show us the Father and we shall be satisfied.
Have I been with you all this time, Philip, and you do not know me. I am the Father. The Father is the 'I am' in all.
Philip: Lord, it seems I am different from whom I think I am?
Who do you think you are?
Philip: I am Philip.
This is only a name. It is like a label. Did you come into this world with any name?
Philip: My parents gave me my name.
Yes, all the names you have now had been given to you after your birth. People identify you by your name. However, you do not identify yourself by your name. You may be resting and a visitor may enquire, "what are you doing, Philip?" You would not say to him, "Philip is resting". Rather you would reply, "I am resting". The reason is that your true name is 'I am'. Try to inquire into the nature of this 'I am.'

When you say, "My Name" or "My handkerchief", it means that you are different from the name or handkerchief. In addition, when you say, "my body", it means that you are distinct from the body.[2] The 'I am' is beyond name although it is called by so many names. In the same way, the 'I am' lives in the body but transcends the body. Even when a part of the body is amputated, the 'I am' still maintains its identity as 'I am'. Who is this 'I am' that is beyond name and form?

Philip: Lord, it is hard to define it.

Yes, you can neither define nor confine the 'I am', because it is not finite and it is beyond time and space. You cannot use what is finite, namely the human mind, to comprehend what is infinite, namely the human Spirit. The question, "who am I?" is a quest into the reality of the questioner. It is the end of all questions. You cannot answer this question, as any answer you may provide is wrong. Hence, the 'I am' is the one who provides the answers to every question. Another outside itself cannot solve its mystery. It is its own solution. The 'I am' gives definition to everything but another outside itself cannot define its reality. It is its own definition. Therefore, Self Knowledge happens not by 'knowing' but by being aware; not by 'questioning' but by silence.

Thaddeus: Lord, while you were teaching the crowd, you said that the gate to the Kingdom of God is narrow and only a few enter through it. What is this narrow gate?[3]

The Kingdom of God is realized through the middle path, which is narrow. When you become aware of the consciousness in the interval between the waking state and the sleeping state, between two consecutive thought waves, between the inhalation and exhalation of breath, between two succeeding heartbeats and between two consecutive ticks of time, you will know the Truth of the Kingdom of God. You will know your Self as that which is beyond life and death, good and bad, male and female, light and darkness, time and space, knowledge and ignorance and all the pairs of duality. You will know your Self as that which has no opposite. As the Buddha would say, "Knowledge lies in the middle".[4]

Magdalene: Master, how can one enter into this kingdom?

The Kingdom of God is not a place you can enter. It does not admit of observation since there is no second outside it to say 'Look, here it is!' or 'Look, it is over there!'[5] The Self which is the Kingdom is all that is. Since there is no one outside the Self, where is the other to find it? And since there is no place outside the Self, why go from place to place searching for it? Be still and know your Self. This is all that is required to realize the Kingdom of God. Silence happens immediately the 'I am' remains alone as 'I am'.

Thomas: What is the difference between Spirit and Matter?

When you know the Self, you will realize that there is no real difference between Spirit and matter. When the 'I am' remains alone as the 'I am', it is called Spirit. This is the stillness of silence. When the 'I am' projects itself as 'I am this or that', it is called matter. Spirit is silence. Matter is sound. Just as sound is born from the womb of silence and dies in the tomb of silence, matter is born, sustained and dissolved back into silence. Like the ocean and its waves, silence and sound are not different. You are the deep blue ocean which is not separate from its waves. You are the silence which is the source of every sound.[6]

Philip: How did creation come about?

Creation occurs through Self-projection, (or objectification). The mind is the power with which the Self objectifies itself as matter. The mind is constantly busy creating and recreating the Self as images of the Self. There is no creation without the mind. What you experience as creation is nothing but the reflection, resound and reaction of the Self. Whatever you see as object is a reflection of the Self. What ever you hear as sound is a resound of the Self and whatever you experience as action is the reaction of the Self.

Simon: Master, how can the knowledge of God make one become God?

You do not become God. You are already that, now. There was never a time when you were not God. Divine knowledge makes you realize what you have always been. The 'I am' is not something which is attained in the future. It is not something which is realized by prescribed actions and inactions. You are that already without any need to do anything. You only forgot your Divinity when you projected your Self as images of your Self. The moment you relinquish this urge to 'become', to 'project', you will know that there has never been any difference between the knower and the known. Divine knowledge is the awareness that the 'Self' alone is.

34

Part II:
The Law

Within them I shall plant my law, writing it on their hearts... There will
be no further need for anyone to teach another saying, 'Learn to know
Yahweh.' No, they will all know me, from the least to the greatest."
Jeremiah 31: 33-34

The Self is the law, the law giver and the law keeper,
and there is no second to break the law.

3
The Self Alone Is
...There is None Apart

Jesus said to them:
"Hear O Israel, the Lord our God, the Lord is One."
Mark 12:29

One of the teachers of the law got up and put this question to Jesus, *"Master, which is the first of all the Commandments?"* Jesus said to him, *"This is the first: 'Listen, Israel! The Lord our God is one, the only and you must love the Lord your God with all your heart, with all your soul, with all your mind and with all your strength. The second is as the first, you must love your neighbor as yourself. There is no Commandment greater than these."*[1]

The Scribe said to Jesus, *"Well said Teacher, you have spoken the truth, for there is one God, and there is no other but he. And to love him with all the heart, and with all the understanding, and with all the soul, and with all the strength, and to love one's neighbor as oneself, is more than all the whole burnt offerings and sacrifices."*

Seeing how wisely he had answered Jesus said to him, *"You are as far from the kingdom as you are from yourself."*[2] After this, no one dared to ask him further questions.

Afterwards, when he was alone with his disciples, he taught them in details the real meaning of the law.[3]

Peter: Lord, the scribes have made a yoke out of the law. They have taken away the key to Self Knowledge, neither going in nor allowing others to go in.[4]

I have come to restore the essence of the law.[5]

Andrew: Lord, teach us the true meaning of the Ten Commandments as it was given to Moses on the mountain.

What is the first Commandment?

Andrew: "Listen, Israel, Yahweh our God is One, the only. You shall not worship any other God apart from Yahweh".[6]

The word 'Yahweh' means 'I am'.[7] Each time you say 'I am', you are calling the Name of Yahweh. Yahweh, God or 'I am' is Pure Existence. If you rephrase the first Commandment replacing Yahweh and God with 'I am', it will look like this: *"Listen, Oh Israel, 'I am' your 'I am' is One and only. You shall not worship any other 'I am' apart from 'I am'."* This means that God alone is.[8] There is nothing apart from the 'I am'. Your 'I am' is the 'I am' in all. The worshiper is the worshiped. This is the basic law of Moses.

When you think God is separate from you, you create false gods. These gods are false because they are imaginary and the mind is responsible for imagination. This is the reason why the second Commandment warns that you shall not make images of the Self.[9] The mind creates images of the Self and makes you think that the image is the reality. Hence, you cannot arrive at true worship with the mind for *"God is Spirit and those who worship God must worship in Spirit and in Truth."* [10]

Philip: Is the idea of heaven and hell false?

Heaven is where God is and God is everywhere. The opposite is hell. The difference is in Awareness and not in location. When you are aware that God alone is, that is heaven. When you lack this awareness, that is hell.

Peter: I used to think that God is an entity that lives somewhere in the firmaments!

There are three possible wrong understandings of the fundamental Truth expressed so powerfully in the first and most important Commandment of the Bible: *"Listen Oh Israel, God is One and only. You shall not worship any other God apart from 'I am'"*[11]

The first wrong understanding is to think that one's own God is the true God, the One and only, and that the 'gods' of other people are false. There are not many gods, one for each religion among people! God is one. He is Omnipresent. Love is one; it transcends caste, colour and creed. Truth is one; there cannot be two for two can only be one, occurring twice. The goal is one, for all roads must lead to the One God. 'I am' is One.

When anyone says, *"Your God is different from my God"* or *"your religion is different from my religion"*, that person has not understood the fundamental Truth of the oneness of the 'I am'.

The second misconception is to see God as different from his manifestations. This misconception arises from the illusion that seeks to separate that which is inseparable. Like the sun and its rays, the ocean and its waters, the tree and its branches, God is not different from his creation, although God is beyond his manifestations. God is the existence from which all things derive their existence. Everything that is, is in God because God alone is.

'I am' is the first and the last, the outward and the inward. In '*I am*', all live, move, and have their being.[12] Everything is God, yet God is beyond the totality of everything.

Thomas: This is hard to believe Lord. Does it mean that the chair I am sitting on is God?
The chair is God; however, God is beyond the chair. What you actually see as 'chair' is nothing but vibration energy emanating from the womb of 'I am'. It is like a ripple from the heart of Silence. It emerges and merges back like a wave of energy in the ocean of existence. The wave is part of the ocean but the ocean is bigger than the wave. Yet the two are inseparable. In the same way, the chair is a spark of the 'I am' but 'I am' is beyond the chair, yet both are inseparable. As far as that chair exists, it exists in God and as far as it exists in God, it is God.

The unity of the 'I am' and creation is like the unity that exists between the tree and its parts. 'I am' is the vine and creation is its branches,[13] leaves, roots and fruits. This big tree, which has so many different components and so many different parts, is really one in the sense that the seed is only one.[14] Just as there is only one seed for the entire tree, there is only one divine 'I am' and all other parts are essentially related to this one source.

'I am' is the one supreme, which contains everything in the

universe. 'I am' is the seed of all beings. Just as you are witnessing all the different forms and parts of the tree, although they have arisen from the same seed, so also you are experiencing different aspects of the one God. God is only one; there is nothing outside of him.

The third wrong understanding of the first commandment is to see God as different from oneself. If Yahweh is the 'I am', how can one say 'I am' different from 'I am'? Again, it is this sense of difference that creates what the scriptures call, 'false gods'.[15] When you think, 'I am separate from I am' you create an illusion, which seeks to separate that which is inseparable and to join that which was never apart. [16]

Magdalene: Are you saying Lord that we are not different from God!
The moment you realize the 'I am' within you, at that instant you will know that there is indeed none apart from the 'I am'. Treat everyone as the tabernacle of the living Christ. See yourself in all because you are the 'I' in all. This outlook will change your attitude towards all. It will transform all your work into worship. Everything you do will be done in Christ, through Christ and for Christ. This is the worship of the true God.

When you worship the objects of your mental creations such as fame, money, sex, food, alcohol, addictions, the list is endless, these mental creations become 'false gods' and prevent you from knowing your true Self.

Martha: How can one go beyond this sense of separation?
Go beyond the image. This is the meaning of the second part of the first commandment.

4
Beyond Images
...The Self is Known

Jesus said to the Samaritan woman:
"God is Spirit, and those who worship must worship in Spirit and Truth."
John 4:24

Jesus was sitting alone by the well of Jacob, his disciples having gone to the town to buy food, when a Samaritan woman came up to draw water. Jesus said to her, "Give me some water." The woman hesitated because the Jews were not allowed to mix with Samaritans.[1] Jesus said to her, "If you only knew the gift God is offering to you and who it is that is saying to you 'Give me something to drink,' you would have been the one to ask, and he would have given you that living water which when you drink it you will never be thirsty again." The woman replied, "I see you are a prophet. Our fathers worshiped on this mountain, though you say that Jerusalem is the place where one ought to worship." Jesus said, "The time is here when you will worship the Father neither on this mountain nor in Jerusalem. God is Spirit, and those who worship must worship in Spirit and Truth."[2]

At this point his disciples had returned and were surprised to find him speaking with a Samaritan woman.

Thaddeus: How can one worship God only in spirit?

Go beyond the image. This is the meaning of the second part of the first law of Moses which says, *"You shall not make images of Yahweh (the 'I am')"[3] The law further states that: "You shall not make yourselves an image or any likeness of anything in heaven above or on earth beneath or in the waters under the earth."[4]* That is to say, you shall not make an image of the 'I am' in the three states of the mind – waking, dreaming and sleeping. To realize the first law, you must go beyond the mind.

It is not possible to keep the first (that is, true worship of Yahweh or the realization that God alone is) without the second (going beyond images / mind).

Thomas: Why is it forbidden to make images of the 'I am'? Is creation itself not the image of God?

Creation is the image of God, however to know God, you have to go beyond his image. For example, the beautiful picture of your mother reminds you of her whenever you look at it. This image also evokes a feeling of love and longing in your heart to be with your real mother. However, no matter how much you cherish and adore this picture, it can never give you the experience of your living mother. To confuse the reality of your mother with her image is the idolatry, which this commandment wants to eliminate. Idolatry happens when the real appears to you as unreal and when you mistake the unreal for the real. In the same way, what you see in the gross and mental worlds are only images of the 'I am'. To experience the truth of yourself, you must go beyond physical and mental images. The physical is a reflection of the mental and the mental is a reflection of the spiritual. The Spirit is the source.

Bartholomew: Lord, does this mean we should do away with all idols and the use of other ritualistic objects in our prayers?

It is very easy to do away with physical images; however, the real hurdle in the knowledge of the Spirit is to remove the images of the mind. Without removing the mental images, the physical images will always persist. This is because the physical is a reflection of the mental. As long as the mirror of the mind is there, images are inevitable. When the mind disappears, what remains is the 'I am', (reality).

Thomas: How is it possible to remove the images of the mind?

A man tying to remove the images of the mind is like a man fighting with his own shadows. It is a futile effort. The more you try to 'remove' them, the more you make them look real. Hence, all that is required is to know the true nature of the mind. In this awareness, there is nothing to move or remove. Beyond effort and effortlessness, you will remain in the state of unattached stillness. In silence, you will realize the essence of the first Commandment and the quintessence of the other nine.

Andrew: Master, how is it possible to worship God without images? Religion itself is synonymous with images, whether physical or mental. Language and words are part of imagination. How can we communicate with the Divine without these essential aids?

The second Commandment forbids the images of 'I am' because it is not possible to realize the 'I am' on the level of images. The mind is pure 'imagi-na-tion'. To realize God, you must go beyond images in the form of thoughts, concepts, ideas, memory, language, intelligence, and will. To know your Self, you must enter into absolute silence.

However, in the earlier stages of spiritual growth, the use of images may be indispensable. Suppose you want to teach the word 'table' to a small child. If you merely utter the word 'table' it does not become clear to him what this image is. However, you can show him a table and ask him to look it over carefully. While he is doing this, you repeat the word 'table'. The image of the particular table you used to teach him the meaning of the word may be impermanent (that table may change); but the word 'table' and the type of objects it represents will remain. One can understand the permanent element through the impermanent. Therefore, though Divinity is imageless, in the earlier stages of religion you have to associate it with a particular image to understand it.

Matthew: So it is not a sin to use images.

Little children need to learn with the help of big letters scrawled on boards and slates. Temples, churches, dogmas, creeds, idols, rosaries, statues, flowers, incense, oils, candles, sacramental, and other ritual objects are the slates and boards, for children in spiritual progress. The word 'Spirituality' comes from two words, 'spirit' and 'ritual'. When you remove the ritual what remains is pure Spirit. However, you cannot arrive at pure Spirit without going through the rituals.

People pass through servant-hood, son-ship and Godhead[5] for the supreme realization of the oneness of the Self. Servant-hood is the spiritual stage where one sees God as a reality separate and outside from oneself. Here, one's attitude is that of 'Listen Lord your servant is speaking'. Because the worshiper is seen as different from the worshiped, the use of images and rituals is predominant in this stage.

The perfection of this stage is when the worshiper sees the worshiped not just in the particular images and symbolisms of her own religion but also in every form in the universe. She sees God in people, animals, trees, the sun, the soil, the rain, the river and in everything. She worships, loves and serves God in creation. This universal worship leads her to the second stage where she begins to see God within herself. She begins to see herself also as an image of God.

The second stage is the son-ship. Here the worshiped is within the worshiper. The relationship is that of the father and his son or the mother and her daughter. There is a strong feeling of intimacy, an inseparable bond in the heart of the worshiper, which makes him realize that God is closer to him than his very breath. He feels strongly that "The Father is in me and 'I am' in the Father". He addresses God as "Abba – Father"[6]. He sees himself as the "Son of God"[7] or "Child of God".

At this stage, there is an intense longing for mystical union. The only thought in the heart of the worshiper is the thought of the beloved. All her desires have been sublimated in the one desire for the Lord. Like the drowning person gasping for the last breath, her soul languishes in the pangs of separation from her beloved, as words and images no longer satisfy her. Solitude becomes her sole companion and only refuge. She cannot live a moment without the thought of the Lord. She is ready for the final birth.

The ultimate stage is when the worshipper realizes himself as the worshiped. "The Father and I are One"[8] is the final realization of the 'I am'. This knowledge is realized in absolute silence beyond physical and mental images, and you are then aware of the infinite potential of the 'I am' principle.

5

You are the 'I am'
… The Infinite Potential

Jesus said to them:
Whatsoever you do to anyone, you do it to me[1]
Matthew 25:40

The Scribes and Pharisees brought a woman along who had been caught in the very act of committing adultery. They made her stand in the middle and said to Jesus, "Master, this woman was caught in the very act of committing adultery, and in the law Moses ordered us to stone women of this kind. What have you got to say?" Jesus, who was writing on the ground with his finger, straightened up and said, "Let the one among you who is guiltless be the first to throw a stone at her." Then he bent down and continued writing on the ground. When they heard this they went away one after the other until Jesus was left alone with the woman. Jesus again straightened up and said, "Woman, where are they? Has no one condemned you?" "No one sir," she replied. "Neither do I condemn you", Jesus said to her.[2]

When the woman had gone, the disciples raised up questions concerning what had happened.

James: Lord, why didn't you condemn the woman?

I see my Self in her. When you condemn 'another', you condemn yourself since you are the same Self in the 'other'.

Judas: Why do people commit sin?

Because they think they are sinners. You are whatever you attribute to the 'I am'. This is the essence of the second commandment which says, "*You shall not misuse the Name of Yahweh your God!*"[3]

You misuse the Name of Yahweh, the 'I am', whenever you attribute evil to the 'I am'. For example, whenever you say, 'I am weak', 'I am stupid', 'I am poor', 'I am sick', 'I am sinful', 'I am damned' and such things, you bring the Name of Yahweh into misuse. The scripture says, *"Yahweh (I am) would not hold him innocent that takes his Name in vain."*[4] This is because by saying 'I am weak', you become weak. Poverty becomes your property, when you say 'I am poor'. You shall never be free from sin when you feel, 'I am a sinner'.

The 'I am' is the infinite potential of all possibilities and it will materialize whatever you attribute to it. The 'I am' is neither positive nor negative, neither good nor evil. Instead, the 'I am' takes on your positive or negative affirmations. If you attribute goodness to it, it is supreme goodness. If you attribute evil to it, it is the great destroyer. Choose good and you are God or choose evil and you are the devil. God and devil reside within the 'I am'. What you call 'devil' or 'Satan' is nothing but the misuse of the 'I am'. In the scriptures, 'Satan' is referred to as one of the 'Sons of Yahweh'.[4] Hence, all powers and forces are derived from the 'I am' and none can operate above or beyond the 'I am'.

For example, the fire element contains within itself the power of both life and death. You cannot say it is a product of Satan because it can destroy whole cities and turn them into ashes because of the bad will of man. This is true of all the elements. Everything has within it the fullness of blessing and at the same time the fullness of curse depending on their use or misuse.

Dear Children of Immortality, awaken the divine powers of the 'I am' within you. Affirm the splendor, glory, majesty, honor, and beauty of the 'I am' and that you are. Be aware of 'I am' as not different from God. I am Spirit. I am Truth. I am Love. I am Peace. I am infinite abundance. I am eternal righteousness. I am free. I am fearless. I am existence, knowledge, and bliss. I am the infinite potential of all possibilities. I am omnipotent, omniscient and omnipresent. I am in all. All are in me. I pervade this universe. I am Christ. I am Krishna. I am Buddha. I am Divine!'

Nicodemus: What does scripture mean when it says, "do to no one what you would not want done unto you?"[6]

It means, "All are one. Be alike to everyone." Since there is no 'other' outside your 'Self', whatever you do, you do it only to your Self. When you say to someone, 'you are a fool', you are simply saying to yourself, 'I am a fool'.[6] When you bless someone, you are only blessings yourself. When you do something, do not feel you are doing it to another. Feel you are doing it to yourself. Then, the feeling of oneness will become spontaneous. You will naturally treat and love your neighbor as your Self only when you see your Self in your neighbor.[8] Love of the 'Self' is the essence of all the commandments. When you realize this essence, you will know the meaning of the Sabbath.

6
The Essence of the Sabbath
...is Silence

Jesus said to them:
"The Sabbath was made for man, not man for the Sabbath. So the Son of
Man is master even of the Sabbath."
Mark 2:27-28

While Jesus was teaching in the synagogue, a man was there whose right hand was withered. The Scribes and Pharisees were watching him to see if he would cure somebody on the Sabbath. Knowing their thoughts Jesus said to the man with the withered hand, "Get up and stand in the middle!" And Jesus said to them, "I put it to you, is it permitted on the Sabbath to do good, or to do evil; to save life, or to destroy it?" Then he said to the man, "Stretch out your hand." He did so and his hand was restored.[1]

And when he was alone with his disciples, they asked him questions concerning the third commandment of Moses.

Andrew: Lord, it seems that the teachers of the law do not understand the true meaning of the Sabbath.

What does the law say about the Sabbath?

James: "Keep the Sabbath day Holy. For in six days the Lord made the heavens and the earth, the sea, and all that is in them. But on the seventh day he rested, and blessed the Sabbath and made it holy."[2]

The Sabbath is the state of rest. The teachers of the law thought that keeping the Sabbath meant abstaining from activity (work). However, it is not possible to desist from action because the body-mind complex is a bundle of activities. Whether in the waking, dreaming or sleeping states, one is engaged in activity: breathing, walking, eating, thinking, dreaming, and so on. To rest from activity (that is, to keep the Sabbath holy) does not mean to abstain from work but to experience that 'silence' which is the source of every

47

activity, that 'stillness' which is the cause of every movement and that 'nothingness' which is the seed of everything. That 'rest' is the peace of the soul and the soul is restless until it realizes the Sabbath.

Although the Sabbath is the source and sustenance of every activity, it is eternally silent. Though it is perpetually working, it is forever at rest. Even though it is perennial eloquence, it is the background witness. Like the screen of creation, the Sabbath is unaffected by the activities projected on it. Yet without it, the whole of creation will collapse. The Sabbath means Self-awareness and is beyond the body-mind complex, time and causation, being and becoming, effort and effortlessness. The one who is aware of the Self is master of the Sabbath.

When the scriptures assert that God made the cosmos in six days and rested on the seventh, they are referring to the six modifications of the One or how the One became six and how the six lead to the One. In the sacred Cabbala, the Sabbath is the seventh church, the sanctuary of silence, the sanctum sanctorum or holy of holies where God dwells in the cave of the heart. It is only in the Seventh that one can realize the Self. Through the six modifications, one is lead from creation to the creator, from time to eternity, from work to rest, from sound to silence, and from the many to the One.

In the Hindu religion, the Sabbath is related to the Vedic classification of the seven chakras or energy centres, which have their points of correspondence along the cerebrospinal system.[4] The first chakra has its centre at the base of the spine. It is the seat of Eve, or the latent cosmic energy coiled like the ancient serpent at the coccyx, waiting to be raised up on the 'rod' of Moses.[4]

The second has its door at the sacral, opposite the generative organs. It is the treasure chest of the subconscious mind.

The third has its gate at the lumbar, at the region of the navel. It is the seat of the life principle within the human body.

The fourth has its door at the solar plexus opposite the heart. It is the seat of the breath of life.

The fifth has its centre situated in the region of the throat. It is the seat of the Holy Spirit or the Word of God (Creative Word).
The sixth has its door located at the centre of the forehead, between the eyebrows. It is the seat of Christ consciousness.

Finally, the seventh, which is the Sabbath, has its door located one fingerbreadth above the crown of the head. It is the seat of the 'I am that I am' or God consciousness. When the seal of the seventh gate is broken, one will experience Silence.[5] The kingdom of the world will become the kingdom of God.[6]

Originally Moses was given only one law – the law of love which states that the Self alone is. This law was carved on the tablet of the human heart. That is why everyone points to the heart (the principle of love) when referring to the Self.

When the people could not keep the original law, Moses 'broke' it at the foot of the mountain.[6] They could not understand the language of oneness because they were still living in duality. Moses returned to the mountain and pleaded for a modification of the original law.[8] Hence, the One was modified into ten. Truly, the Ten Commandments are commentaries on the law of love. As time went on, even these ten were multiplied into so many laws as the scribes piled up commentaries upon commentaries until the law became a heavy burden, which instead of aiding the knowledge of the Self, prevented it.

The Christ took this form to restore the original law[9] which is simple and single. The new Commandment, which I give you – Love one another as I have loved you[10] – is actually not new. It is ancient and eternal. It is the foundation of creation. Love has no birth, nor death. It knows no reason and adheres to no season. If you follow the law of love (that the Self alone is), you do not need any other law. You are the law itself since you are the Self. The time is here, when "the earth shall be full of the Knowledge of the Lord (that is Self Knowledge) as the water cover the sea."[11] This will be the age of the 'I am' consciousness where people will live in the unity of Divinity. There will be no one to break the law because there will be no one who is not aware of the Self.

Thomas: Lord, how are the Ten Commandments modifications of the first law?

The law is one: the Self alone is.[12] The other nine, thou shall not misuse or make images of the Self, keep the Sabbath holy, honor your father and mother, do not kill, do not commit adultery, do not steal, do not bear false witness, do not covet your neighbor's goods, and do not covet your neighbor's wife, are derived from the basic law.[13]

For example, when you realize the first law, which states that God alone is, you will regard father and mother as God. Self-respect is when you honor everyone as the Self. Again, the fifth law forbids you to hurt anyone in thought, word or deed. When there is only one, who is killing who? There is no 'second' to hurt another. When you see your Self in everyone, how can you cause harm to anyone? The moment you realize that you are in all and all are in you as the same Self, you will spontaneously love all as yourself.

The sixth commandment is also derived from the first. One who has realized the oneness of the Self is ever established in the bliss of the Self. He is married to the Self in divine union. He or she may or may not choose to engage in sexual relations. However, when they do, they become living examples of the power of chastity in married life.

The rest of the laws are also derived from the first. One can only steal or covet when one is living in duality. The moment you realize you are the One, who is stealing from who? The idea of theft, covetousness, or false witness is only possible when there are two. However, the basic law says there is only One.

Part III:
The Negation of the Opposites

Jesus said to them:
From the beginning God made the two one. They are no longer two but one. So what God has united, no one must divide.[1]
See Matthew 19:3-6

As long as one feels there is 'another' apart from the 'I am', one cannot escape the immutable law of duality.

7
Your True Self
...is Beyond Reincarnation

Jesus said to Peter:
*"Put your sword back, for all who draw the sword
will die by the sword."* [1]
Matthew 26:52

One day Jesus took his close disciples, Peter, James and John up on a high mountain. There Jesus revealed to them a glimpse of His Divine effulgence. As the men watched Jesus was transfigured. His appearance changed so that His face shone like the brilliance of a million suns, and His clothing became dazzling white. Suddenly, Moses and Elijah appeared and began talking with Jesus. Peter blurted out, "Lord, this is wonderful! If you want me to, I will make three shrines, one for you, one for Moses, and one for Elijah." This Divine experience was too much for Peter and he wanted it to be permanent. But even as he said it, they were taken up in a cloud of bliss. In this Super-conscious state they heard the Primordial Sound of Silence saying: "This is My beloved Son, and I am fully pleased with Him. Listen to Him." This heightened experience gave the disciples a spiritual shock. They fell face down on the ground. Jesus, the all compassionate Mother came and resuscitated them. "Get up," He said, "Do not be afraid." With His gentle touch, the disciples came back to normal consciousness and when they looked they saw only Jesus with them.[2]

Jesus said to them, "Do not to tell anyone about your experience until the resurrection when the world will know that I have power to lay down this body and power to take it up again."[3]

This Divine experience instilled in the hearts of the disciples the truth of the Divinity of their Master. "Yes, He is the promised Messiah, the One who is to come". However, one more doubt lingered in their minds. The prophets of yore had given unmistakable signs that will herald the coming of the Anointed One. One of these is that the great Prophet Elijah, who lived 850 years ago, will come again to prepare the way for the Messiah. "Behold I will send you Elijah the Prophet before the coming of the great day of the Lord".[4] "Since this prophecy has not been fulfilled", the disciples wondered in their minds, "Why does Jesus claim to be the Promised Messiah?" And as they descended the mountain, they mustered the courage to ask Him.

James: Why do the teachers of religious law insist that Elijah must return before the Messiah comes?[5]

Elijah came in the person of John the Baptist but the people did not recognize him.[6]

Thomas: Why did John the Baptist deny that he was Elijah?[7]

He was unaware of his past lives. Self-ignorance is the cause of rebirth. Self-ignorance is also the reason why one forgets ones past births.

Thomas: What is the cause of this ignorance?

The projection of the Self as 'I am this or that' (or the identification of the Self with objects) is the cause of ignorance. As long as you identify yourself as the body, you can never escape the cycle of birth and rebirth. Reincarnation is an illusion created by body identification. Your true Self is beyond reincarnation. The 'I am' does not come and go because it is omnipresent. Since the 'I am' is never born, how can it die? When it cannot die, how can it be reborn?

Philip: If the Self does not appear or disappear, what is it that reincarnates – the body or the soul? If it is the body, why is John's body different from that of Elijah? If it is the soul, what is the difference between the Self and the soul?

Bodies are always changing. The body you are wearing now is not the same body you had as a child. Hence, even in the present life, your body goes through many births, that is, body changes. Reincarnation relates to the changes of the body. Soul is individualized Self. There is no essential difference between the air inside a balloon and the air outside the balloon. The Self is like the universal wind. The soul is as the wind trapped inside the balloon. The body-mind complex is the balloon. When the balloon bursts, the wind inside merges with the wind outside and every sense of separation disappears. Reincarnation happens when the Self identifies itself with the body-mind complex. As long as you think you are the body, the cycle of birth and rebirth is inevitable. However, you are not the body and so there is no reincarnation. The purpose of the soul is to know itself as that which was never born and which will never die. This realization is called Self Knowledge.

Joanna: Lord, are the consequences of past actions obstacles towards the realization of the Self?

Do not worry about past lives. The present is all you need because the Self is realized in the present. The mind takes you away from this presence. Forget the past. It is an illusion born from the delusion of self-ignorance. Do not worry about the future because it does not exist. Abide in the now. The mind which is responsible for reincarnation cannot endure in the now. The mind lives in the past and in the future. The Self lives in the now. Once you abide in the present, you are immune from the past. In silence, you destroy the overall consequences of past actions.

Joachim: How can you prove to us that John was truly the Elijah come back to life? This might help us to appreciate the teaching that the reason for birth is to go beyond the cycle of birth and rebirth.

Why do you want to entangle yourself with the intricacies of fate and freewill, action and reaction, suffering and death? Do not seek to be born again. Rather, know your Self as that which is beyond birth and death. "Seek first the kingdom of God and every other thing will be added unto you."[8] All you need is to know the Self. This is the purpose of human birth. Until this end is realized, rebirth is certain. For this reason Elijah the Tishbite was reborn as John the Baptist.

If you look at the lives of John and Elijah from the perspective of duality (cause and effect), it will become clear to you how both lives were but one script acted out in different scenes. John's conception and birth was a miracle. His father, Zechariah, a member of the priestly order of Abijah, was the Temple High Priest when Herod was King of Judea.[9] His mother, Elizabeth, was also from the priestly line of Aaron. Both of them were upright in the sight of God. However, they had no children, because Elizabeth was barren; and they were both well on in years.

One day while Zechariah was engaged in his priestly duties in the temple, he had an unusual experience. The angel Gabriel appeared to him with this message: "Your wife Elizabeth will bear you a son, and you are to give him the name John. He will go on before the Lord, in the spirit and power of Elijah, to turn the hearts of the fathers to their children and the disobedient to the wisdom of the righteous - to make ready a people prepared for the Lord." [10]

This was how John was conceived. He was my first cousin and spent his life in the wilderness teaching the people about the 'Christ' and his mission.[11] The people came to him in numbers and he baptized them in the river Jordan. He told them about another baptism, the 'Christ' baptism which endures on one the knowledge of the Self. John baptized with water but the 'Christ' would baptize with fire and the Holy Spirit. Water could cleanse only the outside, however, the spiritual agent of fire, which represented Christ's baptism, made the inside one with the outside. When everything is cast into the flames of the Holy Spirit, that essence which remains, indestructible, is the 'I am' principle.

When at last, the 'Christ' appeared on the scene, John said to the people, "Behold the Lamb of God".[12] John was surprised when I came to him for baptism in the river Jordan. He knew I was clean inside and outside and had no need for baptism. However, to teach humanity the necessity of spiritual initiation on the path of liberation, I obliged him to baptize me.

After my baptism, John considered his work done. He persuaded some of his disciples to follow me. From then onwards he withdrew from the scene.[13] It was at that time that King Herod seized him and threw him into prison. Herod[14] hated John with the venom of a viper because John had told him, "It is not lawful for you to have your brother's wife."[15] Herod had snatched away Herodias, the wife of his brother Philip while Philip was still alive and thereby violated the Jewish law that forbade the marriage of a man to his brother's wife.[16] John openly denounced this marriage. As a result, Herodias nursed a grudge against John and persuaded Herod to kill him. However, Herod restrained from killing John because all the people believed he was a prophet. As a compromise to his wife, he had him put in prison.[17]

While John was in prison, he was surprised that the 'Christ' was silent about his predicament. He began to have doubts and sent those who came to visit him in prison to ask whether I was the 'Christ' or whether they should keep looking for someone else.[18] Thus, the same John who had said to the people "Behold the 'Christ'" turned round to ask the people, "Is he really the One?"

An opportune moment came for Herodias on the birthday of the King. Herod had invited the high officials, military commanders and the leading men of Galilee for a banquet and Herodias had planned to have her daughter, Salome, dance before Herod and his guests. Salome's dance pleased Herod and his dinner guests and in an impulsive passion, the king promised her under oath of anything she asked for, up to half his kingdom. The little girl went to her mother and said, "What shall I ask for?" The mother replied, "The head of John the Baptist".[19] At once, the girl hurried to the king with the request: "I want you to give me right now the head of John the Baptist on a platter." Immediately Herod regretted his rash promise, but because of his oath and because he did not want to back down in front of his guests, he issued the necessary orders. Suddenly some soldiers came to the prison and cut off the head of John. They brought it on a tray and gave it to the girl, who took it to her mother. Later, the disciples of John came for his headless body and buried it.

Thus ends the story of John's life as the Baptist. As far as the fragmented mind could perceive, it is a very sad story. However, nothing happens in the present without a cause in the past. Caught in the net of duality, none can escape the reactions of the past. Let us now look at the story of Elijah and it will become clear how he was John the Baptist come back to life.

Elijah the Tishbite was one of the greatest prophets Israel ever had and lived during the reign of King Ahab. One of the greatest confrontations he faced during his ministry was the battle for the religious freedom of Israel. Israel worshiped Yahweh, the God of their ancestors and observed the laws of Yahweh, which included the Ten Commandments, and a more extensive list of laws that were written down in the "Book of the Covenant".[20]

King Ahab went against the law[21] and married a foreigner, Jezebel, the daughter of Ethbaal, the King of Sidon. When Jezebel moved to Israel, she brought Baal[22], the God of her people, which she worshiped. As time went on, she forced her husband to make Baal the state religion. Soon, almost all of Israel was worshiping Baal and this violated the religious freedom of Israel. Elijah's mission was to free Israel from the worship of Baal and Queen Jezebel waged a war against this mission.

Because the religious cult of Baal enjoyed the support of the state, it flourished until her prophets grew up to 450. Elijah was the only prophet of Yahweh left. In the end, he was able to convince the King to hold a religious duel between the prophets of Baal and himself. This was to take place on Mount Carmel.

King Ahab gathered all the people and the prophets of Baal together on this Mountain. Elijah told the prophets of Baal in the presence of the people, "You call on the name of your Baal and I will call on the Name of Yahweh; and the one who answers by fire, let Him be God over the people of Israel."[23] The prophets of Baal agreed to this arrangement and all the people said, 'it is well spoken'.

After they had prepared their sacrifice to Baal, they started praying and calling on Baal to come and consume the offering with fire from heaven. They prayed from morning until noon dancing round the altar they had made until they were exhausted. Elijah mocked them saying: "Shout louder! Perhaps Baal is deep in thought, or he is relieving himself. Or maybe he is away on a trip, or he is asleep and needs to be wakened!"[24] So they shouted louder, and following their normal custom, they cut themselves with knives to persuade Baal to answer their prayers. They raved all afternoon until evening, but still there was no answer.

When it was Elijah's turn, he built his altar according to the tradition of the Jewish religion and laid the sacrifice on the altar he had made. He instructed the people to dig a trench round the altar and after they had done this, he commanded them to pour gallons of water on the sacrifice until the altar ran through with water and overflowed the trench. He then walked up to the altar and prayed, "Oh Adonai, God of Abraham, Isaac, and Jacob, prove today that you are God in Israel and that I am your servant. Prove that I have done all this at your command." Immediately the fire of the Lord flashed down from heaven, burned up the sacrifice, the wood, the stones, and the dust, and licked up all the water in the ditch! When the people saw this, they fell on their faces and cried out, "Yahweh is God! Yahweh (I am) is God!"[25]

However, Elijah went beyond bounds and said to the people, "Seize all the prophets of Baal. Do not let a single one escape!" The people seized them all, and Elijah took them down to the valley of Kishon and there he cut off their heads.[26] This act was a breach of the agreement, which he made with the prophets of Baal.[27] This was also not the will of Yahweh. Elijah succumbed to the temptations of religious fanaticism by resorting to violence.

When Queen Jezebel heard what Elijah had done to the prophets of Baal, she vowed to put an end to his life. Jezebel sent a messenger to Elijah saying, "So let the gods do to me and more so, if I make not your life as one of them (the prophets of Baal) by this time tomorrow."[28] Jezebel had this desire ingrained in her mind. From then onwards, she pursued Elijah to end his life. Elijah prayed to

God as he ran away from the hands of Jezebel. He fled for forty days and forty nights to Mount Sinai, the mountain of God and there he had an experience of God's presence. He was not to die in the hands of Queen Jezebel in that lifetime.

There are three reasons, which are responsible for rebirth. One is one's sins, the second is unfulfilled desires and the third is ignorance of the Self. Queen Jezebel could not fulfill her desire to kill Elijah in that present lifetime. She had to be born again as Herodias to carry out her wish. Hence, Herodias' hatred for John the Baptist sprang from her past desire to kill him. The residues of forgotten desires accumulated from past lives make an impact on one's character and personality. King Ahab also returned as Herod and just as he went against the law to marry Jezebel, a foreigner, he went against the law to marry Herodias, the wife of his brother Philip.

As long as one feels there is 'another' apart from the 'I am', one cannot escape the immutable law of duality (action and reaction). This is what Scriptures mean when it says, "all who draw the sword will die by the sword,"[29] "He who sheds the blood of another, by another shall his blood be shed,"[30] "What you sow is what you reap."[31] The effects of certain actions may take many lifetimes to manifest. Nevertheless, one must pass through its purifying tunnel to learn the lesson that there is none apart from the Self.

As long as the illusion of body identification persists, you think there is 'another' to be killed. Like the dog who barks at his own reflection in a mirror, you 'kill' yourself thinking you are 'killing' another. Will the image of the dog disappear even if it barked at it for a hundred years? On the other hand, the dog will cease barking the moment it becomes aware that what it sees is only his own reflection. In the same way, you will go beyond reaction the moment you realize that the Self alone is. Then you will know that there is none outside you to 'kill or to be killed.' Beyond good and evil, fate and freewill, action and reaction, birth and rebirth, the Self will abide in itself as the One without a second.

8
Beyond Good and Evil
...Fate and Freewill

Jesus said to them:
"Be perfect just as your heavenly Father is perfect."
Matthew 5:48

As they were going on the way, Jesus met a man who had been blind from birth. He spat on the ground and made a paste with his spittle. He then put this over the eyes of the blind man and told him to go and wash it off in the Pool of Siloam. When the man did this, he came back able to see.[1]

Thomas: Lord, who sinned, this man or his parents, that he should have been born blind?

Neither he nor his parents sinned. He was born blind so that the Glory of God might be revealed in him.[2] If it were his sins, he would not have been cured.

Judas: Are the consequences of sin inescapable?

The grace of God can neutralize the effect of sin but this can happen only when the devotee has totally surrendered to the Lord. When this happens, the Lord takes over his burden. I give rest to those who take refuge in me.[3]

Mary: How can one go beyond rebirth?

The tree of activity is propagated by the seed of desire. The body is born out of desire. Without desire, there is no mind, without the mind, there is no individuation and without individuation, there is no birth. Without birth, there is no death and without death, there is no rebirth. Therefore, desire is the cause of birth and rebirth.

Once born, action is inevitable. Every action has a reaction and every reaction is propelled by desire which is the root of rebirth. Although action is inescapable, desire can be avoided. Hence, action without desire is the secret which destroys the chain of action and reaction, birth and rebirth. Your action is devoid of desire when you give up the seven circumstances of action. These are the 'who', 'how', 'why', 'what', 'when', 'where' and 'whom' of action. These circumstances are the strings of desire, which make an action good or bad.

An action in itself is beyond good and bad. The mind (the seven circumstances) makes it so. These are responsible for the 'morality' of any action. For example, the act of urination is neither good nor bad in itself. However, when one urinates inside the temple everyone will cry sacrilege! In this case, it is not the act of urination, which is the problem, but 'where' it is done. If it were a one-month-old baby, who had performed the same action, people would not frown at it because the 'who' had changed.

'Good' actions will produce good results and 'bad' actions will produce bad results. Since an action in itself is neither 'good' nor 'bad', except when associated with the seven circumstances, when these seven circumstances are removed, the action will loose its moral power. Hence, without the seven circumstances, you are beyond the reach of fate and freewill, good and evil, birth and death and the dualities of the opposites.

Judas: Lord, how can one remove the seven circumstances of action?
Surrender them to me. You have surrendered the 'who' when you give up the 'I' concept (sense of doership). You no longer feel you are the one 'who' makes things happen but the universal 'I am'. When the ego is not there, you no longer cling to the results of action. The idea, 'I have surrendered' also disappears because there is no 'I' to surrender and there is no 'other', to which the 'I' could surrender. This is the realization of the 'I-less Christ' – "It is no longer 'I' who lives but Christ living in me."[4] In this state, actions become spontaneous;

Arising from the Self
for the sake of the Self
With no compulsion to do it

And with no repulsion not to do it
With no eye on the fruit thereof
And with no sense of 'me' and 'mine'
With no awareness of a separate doer
And with no memory of the deed
It is action without reaction

You have surrendered the 'how' when you realize that God is the means through which every action is performed. God is the great provider! With God, all things are possible. When you no longer think about or worry that a situation has not had the desired outcome, you have relinquished the 'how' of every action.

You have surrendered the 'why' when you realize that God is the reason behind every action and his reason is that love which transcends all boundaries. Whatever happens, happens! Accept it as a Divine gift of pure love. You demonstrate that you have not given up the 'why' whenever you feel, "Why is God doing this to me", "This is unfair", or "Why me?"

You have surrendered the 'when' when you realize that God's time is the best for every action, and God's time is the now. Live in the now - without the worries of the past and the anxieties of the future. You have moved away from the present when you ask, "When is this going to happen?", "Why has it not yet happened?"

You have surrendered the 'what' when you realize that God is not only the efficient cause of every action but also the material cause of action. God is the Goldsmith and the Gold, the substance and the essence, the sum and the substratum. God is the totality and you, as the 'I am', are that fullness which has always been perfect. Being is lost in becoming. Be as you are – the perfection.

You have surrendered the 'where' when you are aware that God is the background Presence of every action. Everywhere is in God! In Him we live, move, and have our being.[5]

You have surrendered the 'whom' when you realize that God is the recipient of every action. Whatsoever you do to any one, you do it to the 'I am'.[6] The 'I am' is One and only. Be alike to everyone.

The seven circumstances are the thread with which one weaves the cloth of desire (the mind). When these threads disappear, one remains in the state of desirelessness (no mind). Reincarnation and karma exist only as long as the mind persists. They are mental dreams. The dream goes on as long as the mind is there. The truth however is that you are not the mind. Hence, there is really no reincarnation[7] because your essence, which is the 'I am' is never born and it will never die. The 'I am' is eternal life.

9
Eternal Life
...Beyond Suffering and Death

Jesus said to them:
"I have Power to lay it (this body) down, so I have Power to take it up again"
John10:18

As Jesus and his disciples were coming down the mountain, Jesus began to tell them plainly, what would happen to him in Jerusalem. He said to them, 'This body will suffer at the hands of the leaders, the leading priests, and the teachers of religious law. It will be killed by crucifixion on a cross but I will raise it up again after three days.'[1]

When Peter heard this, he was filled with deep sorrow. How could the Lord suffer such a shameful death? His mind could not take it. His body started to tremble and his mouth became parched. The hairs on his body stood on end. With a fainting heart, Peter pleaded nervously with Jesus. "Heaven forbid, Lord," he said. "This will never happen to you!"[2]

Jesus turned to Peter and said, "Get away from me, Satan! You are seeing things merely from a human point of view, and not from God's." It is my will to go through the crucifixion to teach you how not to suffer in suffering and how not to die in death.

Peter: Lord, I cannot think about life without you by my side! My mind is confused. All my zeal is gone. How would you allow yourself to pass through such a terrible death?

Do not be downhearted, I cannot die, this is the truth. No one dies. There was never a time I was not. There will never be a time I will cease to be. 'I am' eternal, death relates to the physical body. Changes such as birth, growth, maturity, and death pertain to the body and not to the Spirit. The delusion of body identification is the very definition of Satan. This delusion makes you confuse that which is not real as being real. That which is real is eternal, never changing and indestructible.

The body undergoes uncountable transformations[3] from the tiny foetus in the womb to a baby in the cradle, from the little toddler learning how to walk, to a child playing with the toys. From the young boy or girl going to school, to the youth in the beauty of adolescence; from the matured adult in the fullness of life, to the parent lost in raising up a family; from the grandparent wrinkled with old age to the great-grandparent bent double by the call of the tomb! Finally, the body decays. Meanwhile, even as the body undergoes these six-fold changes, birth, growth, maturity, decline, death and decay - the cells that make up the body are constantly dying and replaced by new ones so that after about seven years the whole body has entirely new cells. However, during all these changes the Self which is the 'I am' within you remains the same. Nothing that is impermanent has true reality. To confuse the body, which is impermanent with your true Self, which is Spirit, is the delusion of Self-ignorance. This ignorance is the cause of your depression.

Satan is not any historical figure living in the underworld. Satan is the illusion, which deludes your discriminatory faculty. It makes you think you are mortal whereas who you really are is immortal. It makes you identify yourself with a particular body whereas you are the absolute Spirit. It is the cause of all your sufferings and miseries. Once you are able to conquer this illusion (Satan[4]) and come to the knowledge of your true Self, you will be happy in every circumstance.

Peter: I am attached to your physical presence and it is unthinkable to stay a moment without you!

'I am' not this body. The body is no more than a water bubble, which springs from the ocean of existence and disappears before the wink of time. 'I am' the eternal Spirit who dwells in the temple of every body. 'I am' unaffected by all worldly changes and cannot be wounded by any weapon. 'I am' all pervading, and beyond the dimensions of time and space.

Your present sorrow will cease immediately you realize that the Christ cannot suffer. The Christ cannot die. The Christ is always with you, in you, around you, above you and below you. You are the Christ.

James: Lord, if we cannot die why are we naturally afraid of death?

Because you identify your Self with the body, whose nature is death. This fear will disappear immediately you realize your true Self. The Self cannot die because it was never born. That which cannot die is not afraid of death. Anyone who has transcended the body is free from fear. They are also beyond suffering and death. They cannot suffer even though they may pass through 'suffering'. They do not die even though they may pass through 'death'.

Peter: Lord, please help me. Do you mean you cannot feel any physical pain?

'I am' aware of the pain, not only in this body, which you call 'Jesus' but also in every body. 'I am' the Consciousness in every being. Although I am aware of the pain, I do not suffer from it. If I were to suffer, my joy would be incomplete. However, 'I am' complete joy and do not know what you call sorrow.

Peter: What is the difference between pain and suffering?

Suffering is due to identification with the body. Although 'I am' in everybody, yet I have no attachment to anybody. Because 'I am' in everybody, I know the pain. Because 'I am' not attached to anybody, I do not suffer the pain.

In sleep, you may dream that your son was sick and died. You are overwhelmed with sorrow in the dream. Then you wake up and discover it was a mere dream and suddenly you feel a sense of relief and joy. What is the cause of your sorrow in the dreaming state and your joy in the waking state? It is because of the attachment you have for your son. After all, people die everyday. However, you are unaffected because you have no sense of 'me' or 'mine' towards them. Sufferings disappear immediately you go beyond, 'my body', 'my car', and 'my son' and so on. For example, in deep sleep, that is dreamless sleep, you do not experience any pain or pleasure. Even though you might have gone to bed with a severe pain, once in deep sleep the pain disappears. In deep sleep, the father forgets that he is a father. The king also forgets that he is a king and the pauper, that he is a poor person. All distinctions of class, caste, creed and country, and all identifications with name and form disappear. It is because in deep sleep there is no feeling of 'I' as the seed of the ego is temporally withdrawn. Because there is no ego, there is no attachment and because there is no attachment, there is no suffering. However, as soon as the ego wakes up from the state of deep sleep, the sense of identification with a particular body returns.

James: Lord, how did this ego come about?

The ego is the reflection, resound and reaction of the Self. The Self is 'I am'. The ego is 'I am this or that'. In the statement, 'I am James', James is the ego. When you remove the ego, that is, James, what remains is 'I am', that is, God. You can never experience suffering when you remain in the state of 'I am' as this is your true Self. Try to distinguish between 'what you are' and 'what you have'. 'What you have' ('I am this or that') is the ego. 'What you are', (I am that I am) is the Self. The ego mistakes what you are which is eternal with what you have which is constantly changing.

The moment you give up the sense of 'me' and 'mine', then you are truly free, beyond the 'possessor' and the 'possessed'. 'I am this or that' are the projections of the Self as radiation, vibration and materialization.[5] The identification of the Self with its projections is the root of suffering. When you identify the 'I am' with a name, sorrow overwhelms you when your name is defamed. When you identify the 'I am' with property, you are thrown into grief when the property is stolen, burnt or confiscated. When you identify the 'I am' with relationships, you feel the pangs of separation. When you identify the Self with the body, death will be a torment. The truly wise ones grieve neither for the living, nor for the dead because they have gone beyond the barriers of 'me' and 'mine'.

Self-emancipation is a shift in consciousness, a change of attitude -from 'I am this or that' to 'I am that I am', from the outer to the inner, from sound to silence, from activity to rest and from what you have to what you are.

John: Lord, is suffering inevitable on our journey to God?

You can decide not to suffer right now by removing the sense of 'me' and 'mine'. Then the birth of the Self will know no labor pains. Whenever you suffer, it is because you are clinging to something at that moment. The pain you undergo is a call to let go. It is the caution of the Self, who is the eternal witness of the play of life. When you feel, 'I will only be happy when I get 'this' or 'that' or when 'this' or 'that' is removed from me', you give power to that condition to rule your life and you become a slave to it. The Self can never be sick, sad or in lack. The Self is complete joy. Immediately you identify your Self with your Self, all limiting conditions like sicknesses, poverty or sorrow will disappear. Have faith in your Self and develop Self-confidence. Believe in your Self. Abide in your Self. Realize your Self. Enjoy your Self.

You may experience some joy when you acquire the object of your desire. Nevertheless, this joy is a reflected joy as its real source is the Self. The Self is the generator of joy and this joy passes through a mental transformer, which reflects and transmits it through the objects of the world. Hence, the joys you experience when you come into contact with objects does not come from the objects as such, they are ripples from the Self. The moment you experience the joy of the Self, your joy will be complete.[6] Self joy is joy without objects.

John: Lord, teach us the easiest way to attain the joy of the Self.

There is nothing to attain. Live in this awareness. You are the 'joy of the Self'. This is your true nature. Feel you are the Christ because that is what you are. The dawn of the Christ Consciousness happens spontaneously and you know your oneness with the eternal.

Magdalene: What is the origin of desire?

First, you register an object in your mind through the senses. Second, your mind takes the form of that object as a thought impression. Third, this impression becomes strong by constant churning of the same thought pattern. Fourth, a thought energy field creates itself.

Fifth, you develop 'likes' and 'dislikes' as a result of this thought energy field. An energy field can intensify and expand when the same thought-pattern repeats itself.

Every thought energy field has a magnetic effect. This is the power of attraction or repulsion. Each thought energy field that you create has in it the seed of duality producing the negative and positive poles of the field. The power of the polarity depends on the intensity of your thought energy field. Your intensified thought energy field will either attract or repel you from the object of your sense perception.

This power of attraction (likes) or repulsion (dislikes)[7] is desire. Desire makes you restless by projecting your mind outside the Self. Desire is the urge that creates the delusion that your happiness or sorrows derive from the non-Self. However, beyond sense objectification, your true happiness lies in the silence of the 'I am'.

Part IV:
Silence

"Be Silent and Know that I am God."
Psalm 46:10

Silence is that awareness where there is no 'I' concept.

10
Beyond the Senses
...to the Silence of the 'I am'.

Jesus said to them:
"You shall love the Lord your God with all your strength."
Mark 12:30

While they were at table, Jesus stood up, took off his robe, wrapped a towel around his waist, and poured water into a basin. Then he began to wash the disciples' feet and to wipe them with the towel he had around him.[1]

When he came to Simon Peter, Peter said to him, "Lord, are you going to wash my feet?" Jesus replied, "You do not understand now why I am doing it; someday you will."

"No," Peter protested, "you will never wash my feet!" Jesus replied, "But if I do not wash you, you have nothing in common with me." Simon Peter exclaimed, "Then wash my hands and head as well, Lord, not just my feet!" Jesus replied, "The Feet is the foundation. Once the pillar is strong, the whole edifice will be solid." After washing their feet, he put on his robe again and sat down and asked, "Do you understand what I was doing? All feet are mine. Wash the feet of one another.[2] Whatever you do to any of these, you do it to me[3] since service to man is service to God. Self service is the easiest way to realize the Divinity in humanity. "Self Service" is that service rendered with the awareness that there is none apart from the Self (God).

Bartholomew: Lord, how can one love God with the whole of one's strength?

Loving God with all your strength means dedicating all the activities of the body to the service of the Lord. It means union with God through your actions. In the Hindu religion, this path is called 'Karma Yoga',[4] that is, union with God through the path of self service.

Thomas: How is it possible to dedicate all the actions of the body to the Lord?

The body is a field of action. External forces work upon it on the one hand and on the other, it makes its own input on the environment. The first is passive action and the other is active action. The body receives external stimuli through the five senses (the ears, the skin, the eyes, the tongue, and the nose) and responds to them through the five organs of action (the tongue, the hands, the feet, the reproductive and generative organs and the elimination organ). Therefore, loving God with all your strength means Self-awareness through the five senses and the five organs of action.

The essence of the senses is to go beyond the senses since Self Knowledge is beyond sense perception. You go beyond the senses when every sound, sight, touch, smell and taste draws you inwards to the silence of the 'I am'. In this way, the senses lead you beyond the senses, that is, to the 'I am' presence, which is Omnipresence. This happens when whatever you see moves you beyond the seen and connects you to the Seer, when whatever you hear draws you into the Silence and when whatever you touch transports you into the ecstasy of the boundless Spirit.

Andrew: How does the sense of hearing lead us beyond the sound?

Silence is the source of every sound. The sense of hearing leads you beyond the sound when you are aware of the background stillness behind every sound. You hear the call of the Self in the song of the birds, the whistle of the winds, the roar of the ocean, the cry of the baby, and so on. You are connected to the Silence through the sound, to the unknown through the known, to the inexplicable through the words. You no longer judge whether this sound is good or bad; instead, you perceive every sound as the resound of Silence. You no longer react to words. Rather every spoken word takes you to that Source from where it first emerged.

Peter: How can one go beyond the sense of touch?

You transcend the sense of touch, when every touch brings you into the awareness of God's living presence. You feel the 'I am' in the caress of the cool gentle breeze and the warmth of the rising sun. You know 'I am' there with you in the touch of your loved ones, and when the sprinkles of the morning rain splashes your face as you walk on the street, you know 'I am' the one romancing you. When you feel the 'I am' in everything you touch and in everything that touches you, then you are the master of the sense of touch.

The third sense is the sense of sight. You rise above this sense, when every sight reminds you of the seer. You see your Self in every form, in every face, in every beast and bird, in the sun, the moon and the stars, in the trees, the flowers and the grass. You no longer condemn a sight as ugly and the other as beautiful but you behold every scene as the manifestation of the Self.

The sense of sight is related to the principle of light. If there is no light within you, how can it be there outside? Those who have mastered the sense of sight can control the fire principle. They see beyond the eye because they see with the eye of the 'I'. Like Elias the Prophet, they can command fire from within and transfigure matter into pure energy and energy back into matter.[5]

The fourth sense is the sense of taste. Control of the sense of taste means that you take the right food and in the right proportion. Only then will the body be healthy to serve the indwelling Spirit. Food is God. 'I am' is the life principle in everything you eat. 'I am' the bread of life.[6] 'I am' the living food, which takes away your hunger. 'I am' the living drink, which removes your thirst.[7]

Every meal, which you eat is a 'holy communion' of the Divine presence, for the power of God, the vital force enters into your body through the food. Whenever you sit at the table of the Lord, give thanks and slowly, as a prayer, break the food in your mouth. This is your holy offering in the sacred temple, which is your body.[8] This offering is God, the act of offering is God offered by God in the sacred fire which is God. He alone is God who in all his actions is fully absorbed in God.[9]

Food is the foundation of the spiritual life. Thoughts are the energy equivalent of the food you eat. This means that the subtle part of the food you eat is transformed into thoughts. So the type of thoughts you entertain is largely determined by the type of food you eat, and these thoughts play an indispensable role in your spiritual awareness. The consumed food goes through a long process of digestion, assimilation and conversion into energy. The gross parts of the food are eliminated and the less gross parts build up your muscles and bones. The subtle parts make up the nerves and brains, which are responsible for your moods and thoughts. Hence, you are able to think based on the energy equivalent of consumed food.

The types of food you consume determine your mental purity, the degree of your concentration and the level of your self-control. As the food, so is the head (brain particles). As the head, so is the thought. Your thought influences your moods and your moods control the urges to act in a certain way.[10] Your destiny is largely affected by the type of food you consume.

There are three types of food: foods that create dull thoughts, foods that create passionate thoughts and foods that create serene thoughts.[11] These three types of food relate to the three mental moods or temperaments: sloth, aggression and tranquillity. Those on the path of spirituality should consume foods, which create serene and calm thoughts.

Dull foods are those that make you slothful, sleepy and inactive. They are foods with too much fat and starch. They build up mental moods, which appreciate cold, stale and acrid tastes.

Foods that inflame the passions are foods that are sour, salty or pungent. These are foods based on flesh, fish and all intoxicants, tobacco, drugs and so on. Through intoxicating food, one can lose control over the emotions and passions, the impulses and instincts, and the speech and movements. By eating flesh, one can develop violent tendencies and animal diseases.

Serene Foods are those, which sustain righteous living and keep one light even after the meal. These are vegetables, fruits, grains, leaves, and nuts and food found in their natural states. When you overcook food, you destroy most of the food value in it. For example, when the seeds are fried, they do not sprout. This is a clear proof that the 'life-force' is no longer there. Man is the only living being, who dislikes raw food found in the natural state.

The fifth sense is the sense of smell. You are in control of the sense of smell when you are able to control the vital force in the breath of life. These consist of the five vital airs that activate your body, namely the airs responsible for respiratory, circulatory, digestive, and nervous systems and the air that goes downwards through the canal of your anus.

Stillness is the power through which you tap into the source of the vital force. Silence is absolute breath. In silence, you go beyond the five vital airs and the five senses. The senses are pointers, which direct your focus on the 'I am' principle. Whatever you see, focus on the seer instead of the seen. When you hear a sound, enquire into that which hears. Whatever happens will then direct you to the source, the silence of the 'I am'.

11
Self Service
...Duty without Volition

Jesus said to them:
"Whenever you give alms, your left hand must not know what your right is doing. Your almsgiving must be secret."
Mathew 6:3

Jesus told this story to his disciples. On judgement day, two groups of people will come in the presence of the Father (the I am). To the first group the Father will say, "I was hungry, and you fed me; I was thirsty, and you gave me a drink, I was a stranger and you made me welcome, lacking cloths and you clothed me, sick and your visited me, in prison and you came to see me." They replied, "Lord, when did we ever see you hungry and fed you? Or thirsty and gave you something to drink? When did we see you a stranger and made you welcome, lacking clothes and clothed you? When did we find you sick or in prison and went to see you?" And the Father will reply, "I am the Self in all. Whatever you do to anyone, you do it to Me."[1]

To the second group, the Father would say, "I was hungry, and you never gave me food, I was thirsty, and you never gave me anything to drink, I was a stranger and you never made me welcome, lacking clothes and you never clothed me, sick and in prison and you never visited me." Then they would say with amazement, "Lord, we prophesied and performed many miracles in your name. In your name we fed the hungry, gave water to the thirsty, and clothed the naked. We cared for the sick and visited those in prison."[2] And the Father will reply, "If you had done these for me, you would not have been conscious of them. However, since you kept record of your good deeds, you were doing them for the sake of a reward."

Therefore I tell you, give without expectations - neither for the sake of heaven nor for the fear of hell. When you have done all you have been commanded to do, say, "We are unprofitable servants: we have done that which was our duty to do."[3] In this story, the two groups performed the same type of actions but the first had no expectations attached to their good deeds. Hence they had no memory of them.

Peter: Lord, is it possible to do something good without remembering it?

Do you keep record of the things you do for yourself? This is because you do not expect any rewards when you do things for yourself. For example, when you buy a pair of clothes for yourself, do you expect a compensation for this? However, when you buy the same pair of clothes for 'another', you expect a pile of 'thank you'. As long as you feel there is 'another' apart from the Self, your actions will be reward driven. Immediately you expect rewards from your actions, you will keep record of them like the merchant who keeps a ledger of his debtors. However, if the Self alone is, where is the other to reward another?

This was why the first group were not conscious of their good deeds. They had no sense of 'another' since they were one with the 'I am'.

Martha: Lord, how could the left not to know what the right is doing?

Whatever you do, feel you are doing it to yourself and not to another. Then everything gets done without the memory of the past and the expectations of the future. Expectations can only arise when you feel you have done something for another person. This false feeling of 'another' breeds desires which in turn bind you to the chain of action and reaction. Tossed by the twin twists of pain and pleasure, appointments and disappointments, success and failures, elation and depletion, how can you escape the illusion of duality?

Judas: Can one do evil without an eye to the fruit thereby?

Your action can be 'good' or 'evil', only if you have an eye to the fruit thereby. On the contrary, the actions of those who have relinquished the fruit of action are neither 'good' nor 'evil'. They are beyond any moral evaluation. Since the Self alone is, who is there to judge the other? Can you hurt or help 'another' when you know there is no other?

Martha: Lord, please teach us the easiest way to go beyond the fruit of action.

The five organs of action, the tongue, the hands, the legs, the organ of procreation and the organs of excretion are the principal means through which you perform actions. Be present to every action you perform. To be present means to abide in the now of the action. The moment is full of momentum because it is Omnipresent. Give your full attention to everything you do at every moment. If you are walking, be present to that act of walking. Walk without thought, that is, walk in silence. If you are eating, be present to the act of eating. Eat without thought, that is, eat in silence. If you are brushing your teeth, be present to the contact which the brush makes with your teeth, the sound produced, the taste of the paste, and so on.

You are present when your mind and your body are in the same place at the same time. You lose the power of the now when your mind is disconnected from your body, that is, when your body is in one place and your mind is in another. The body is the home of the mind. When the mind is not at home, you become disconnected from the 'I am' presence. Be in the body then you will be able to go beyond the body. One cannot realize the Self unless embodied. It is only through action that you can transcend reaction.

Martha: Beloved, how can one transcend the body through action?

The body is a bundle of activities. You go beyond reaction when you perform your actions without any attachments. When your actions are without attachments, your right hand does not know what your left has done. You are acting but you do not feel you are acting. It is like the spontaneous action of your heartbeat, your breath of life, or your digestive system. For example, your heart is continuously beating, but you do not feel it is beating. In fact, you become conscious of your heart beats only when you have a heart problem and you develop a heart problem only when your have attachments (worries). In other words, attachment is the disease of action. Beware of this virus. Silent action (Self service) is action without attachment. It is the wellbeing of the universe. The sun is shining without any attachment. The trees are Self giving. The air is just blowing. This is Self service. It has no intention beyond itself. The opposite is trumpet action. It blows trumpets in the synagogues and streets like the hypocrites to call attention to one's acts of charity![4] When you do things for the sake of the 'Self' alone, you are immune from this disease. You are not attached because you do not feel any sense of separation. Whether you are praised or blamed, you are the same, the Self.

Peter: Master, what is it that makes one's actions binding?

Your actions become binding when they are tainted with the sense of doer-ship (the 'I-did' virus) and you feel you are the one who makes things happen. It is this sense of doer-ship that makes you claim the merit or demerit of action. You become attached to the results of your actions. When you understand that you are not actually responsible for the happening of any action, then you will not be affected by the 'I-did' virus. You may think you are responsible for what is happening now. However, what is happening now has only happened because of so many other things that have taken place in the past, of which you are not in control. If you are not in control of the things that must come together to make an action happen, how can you claim the fruits of such an action? Just do your duty and leave the rest to the Power that governs the activities of creation. That Power is your true Self. When you know this Self, you will realize the secret of action without attachment.

John: Are there practical ways in which each of these five organs of action could help in the awareness of the 'I am'?

The first organ of action is the vocal organ. The spoken word is the highest expression of the embodied Spirit. When your words spring from the Silence of the Self, they will vibrate with the power of Truth, and they will give Life.[5] Truth is the harmony between Spirit, thought, and word. Wherever these three agree, there you find the fullness of life.

The heart is the generator of spiritual energy and the hive of every revelation. The heart is another name for silence. Learn to be in tune with your heart. The voice of God can only be heard in silence. When you listen to silence (that is, to your Self), you will hear the voice of consciousness which is the resonance of the 'I am' within every heart.

The Self (Silence) is the embodiment of truth. Speaking from silence is unceasing eloquence. Silence reveals the truth and gives power to the spoken word. Silence makes your word alive and active. Words spoken from silence (Self or heart) bring lasting transformation in the lives of those who listen to them. On the other hand, words spoken through the mind (the head or ego) only give information to those who hear them.

When you are in tune with the heart, the language of Silence will well up within you as formless energy. This energy can be transmitted 'Heart' to 'Heart' without any medium (space-time-body-mind complex). The inspiration of Silence is spontaneous transmission. However, the head can give form to the energy of Silence through the discriminatory faculty (intelligence) as 'information'.

The second organ of action is the hand, which is related to the sense of touch. For example, when an ant is crawling on your skin, you use your hand to remove it. Hence, the hands respond to the sense of touch. In the sensation of touch, the hand is the active sense while the skin is passive. Self service is the best way to transcend this organ of action. Self service is Silent action.

Self service happens when the 'I am' is stripped of the fruits of action, namely name, fame, rewards etc. and you understand that every deed is done by the 'Self', for the 'Self' and through the 'Self'. Feel that the Self alone is. There is no second. Whatever you do, do not feel you are doing it for 'another'; feel you are doing it for your Self.

Peter: Lord, it is so hard for the ordinary mind to believe that those who kill are only killing themselves!

A man who thinks he is killing 'another' is like the dog that jumped into the water in pursuit of its image and got drowned as a result.

Hence the saying, "All those who draw the sword will die by the sword".[6] When you harm others, you are only harming yourself because there are truly no 'others'. Whatever you do, you do it only to yourself because everything is the reflection of the Self. When you bark at your own image in the mirror, wouldn't your image 'bark' back at you? The law, "Do to others, what you would want done to you"[7] is effective only when you realize that there are no 'others'.

These are the three categories of action:[9] First are those who engage in evil actions. Second are those who do good actions but with an eye to the fruits thereof. Lastly are those who perform good actions devoid of its fruits. When you do things for the sake of the Self, naturally, you will not expect any reward. The Self itself is its own reward.

Bartholomew: What is the third organ of action?

The legs are related to the sense of sight. The legs go to where the eyes direct them. This is why a blind person has to be directed to places by another person with a clear sight. Hence, "If one blind person guides another, both will fall into a ditch!" [9]

Walk always in the company of the One with good 'I-sight'. That is, one whose third eye has opened. These are the Masters and Sages who have realized the Knowledge of the Self. To walk in their company is "to walk in the Light of God's Presence".[10] Their mere company[11] will ignite within you a constant awareness of the 'I am'. In every movement be aware of the immovable stillness of the 'I am'. The 'I am' is the unmoving mover of all that is moved. As you walk about, feel the power that moves your legs. Feel the 'I am' stillness and move in the awareness of the immovable Self.

The fourth organ of action is the urinary and reproductive organ. This organ is related to the sense of taste. The tongue is the antenna that receives the taste of food and drink by which the physical body is sustained. The urinary and reproductive organ is associated to the tongue because while the tongue receives water, the urinary organ passes it out; and while the tongue feeds the body through the food, the generative organ produces new bodies.

Chastity is the awareness of the Self in the male and female principle, so that the two shall become One.[12] Every relationship should lead you to Divine union. If you are married, see God in your spouse and love him or her as such. If you choose to remain single, concentrate all your energy on the Self.

The anus is related to the sense of smell. This is evident for obvious reasons! One receives the smell and the other gives it out. The universe is never wasteful. Every form of energy is recycled. See how mother earth transforms your waste, which you dump into her bowels. She turns it into manure. Witness how this manure gives life again to the tree of life, which in turn gives your body its sustenance.

Do not waste food, as food is God. Do not waste water, as water is the life principle. When you respect the water principle in nature, the living spiritual fountain will well up within you. This is the living water which when you drink it you will never be thirsty again because it will take away your thirst altogether.[13] It is the knowledge of the 'I am'.

Magdalene: Sometimes I feel guilty and unworthy. I find it hard to forgive myself.

When the Self alone is, where is the 'other' to forgive 'another'? Truly, the Self has no need for forgiveness. You are the 'I am' and this 'I am' can never be affected by sin as it is ever pure and perfect. Do not associate the 'I am' with sin and you will never be a slave to sin. When you condemn yourself as a sinner, who can free you from sin? When you are the only one who holds the key to your own prison, who can liberate you from your own chains? To condemn the Self as a sinner is indeed the greatest sin![14]

Your negative unconsciousness, this overpowering burden of guilt, makes you unaware of the Self. The truth however is that sin cannot abide in the 'I am' and you are that 'I am'. When you are aware of the limitless Light of the 'Christ' within, there can never be any trace of darkness without. Both cannot co-exist. The secret is remembering God at all times.

12
Remembering God
...at all Times

Jesus said to them:
'You shall love the Lord your God... with all your mind'
Mark 12:30

Jesus went with his disciples to the house of Lazarus in Bethany, a few miles from Jerusalem. Lazarus had two sisters, Martha and Mary. Both loved Jesus dearly. Mary sat at the feet of Jesus, her soul transfixed with the Words that came from him. Martha, who was worried with the serving, came to Jesus and said, "Lord, do you not care that my sister has left all the serving for me. Please tell her to help me."[1]

Jesus said to her, "Martha, Martha, you are concerned and distracted about many things. But only one thing is needed. Mary has chosen it and none can take it away from her. Although it seems to you that Mary is doing nothing, truly she has realized the secret of everything. On the other hand, while you may be seen doing everything, nothing indeed has been done."

Thomas: Lord, if everyone sits and listens to you, who will do the cooking?

You may be sitting at my feet but you are far away from me because your mind is not with me. On the contrary, even though you may be far away, you are dearer than the nearest since your only thought is me. Therefore, whatever you do and wherever you may be, think of me. All you do in Self-forgetfulness is a waste of time and even though you may be seen doing nothing, eternity is added unto time if you remember God. Hence, the essence of work and worship, action and inaction, space and time, sound and silence, is the remembrance of the Lord.

Loving God with your entire mind[2] means remembering God at all times, while awake, while dreaming and while sleeping.

Thomas: How is that possible, Lord?

Fill your mind with love. You cherish anything you love, and you will always think about anything you cherish. With the power of love, your whole mind will vibrate with the Name of God so that in the waking, dreaming and sleeping states, God is the only thought in your mind. With love, you will become aware of God in all circumstances of your daily life - in poverty and in prosperity, in sickness and in health, in success and in failures. The name of God will dance in your heart whether you are at work or at home, openly or secretly, at sea, on the land or in the air. The mind is the vibration of sound. When your mind takes up the resonance of the primal sound (the name of God), it will automatically dissolve in the Self and you will realize your oneness with the One.

The name of God is the root sound or the primal vibration through which everything came into existence.[3] All powers are derived from it.[4] It is the bridge between sound and silence, the known and the unknown. When the mind is completely absorbed with the sacred syllable, you will realize that which is beyond sound.

Mary: Lord, how can one think only of God throughout the day?

The body-mind complex is a bundle of activity. Every activity produces sound and every sound is a resound of the sound of silence. Therefore, every sound produced by the movement of any object is a reverberation of the name of God. The symphony of sounds produced by the activities of the body-mind complex are simply re-echoing the name of God. These activities include, the sound of your thought waves, the sound of your heart beat, the sound of the inhalation and exhalation of breath, the sound produced while eating, bathing, walking, brushing the teeth, or for that matter while sweeping the house or doing other house chores like washing clothes, cutting vegetables, cooking, gardening, and so on. In fact, every sound your body produces or receives is a call to prayer, a signal to remember God.

The aim is to develop the inner ear. When you listen, you will hear the voice of God in every sound produced by every activity of the body-mind complex. For example, the sound produced by your footsteps as you walk along the way is nothing but the resound of 'I am'. Be aware of the 'Self' through this sound. The 'So-ham'[5] sound of the inhalation and exhalation of breath is really an echo of 'I–am'. When you are eating, the sound produced by the clashing and grindings of the molars and premolars and the tearing and biting of the canines and incisors is nothing but the resound of the 'Christ' principle. When you listen, you will hear the name in the crunches and the chomps, the mastication and the swallowing. Then every bite will take you beyond the beat to the One who digests the food within your body in the form of fire.

As you brush your teeth in the morning, listen to the sounds of the brush. They are calling the sacred Name. As you take your bath, listen to the call of the waterfalls on your body. They are re-echoing the Divine Name. The song of the bird is a reverberation of the primal sound. The roars of the ocean are resounds of the first word. The sounds of the raindrops are echoes of the word of God. The whistles of the pines are clarions of Divine expression. In fact, the whole of creation is nothing but the sound of God.

Could you imagine what will happen when you harmonize and integrate the entire sound-producing activities of your body-mind complex during the waking consciousness with the sound of 'I - am'! Your bath will cease to be an ordinary wash but a shower of Divine drizzles of the primordial sound! Your walk will no longer be a mere exercise in transporting the body from one place to another, but a rhythm in the dance of God's Name. Your daily activities will be converted into a rosary of God's Name.

When every association is spent in the remembrance of the 'I am', a spontaneous awareness of God's presence will surround you like a heavenly fragrance welling up from the depth of nothingness. When you enter your bathroom, you will automatically remember God. Your bedroom will become a sanctuary of prayer and your dining room a table of Divine communion. An unseen power will anchor you, making you feel as if you can fly without wings. Your heart will be filled with a Divine music, which is hidden to the ears of mortal man. In short, you will become completely suffused with the ethereal sound that people will think you are intoxicated with the wine of Divine love.

Martha: Lord, the mystics say that the trees talk and that everything speaks.

When your heart is aware of the sound of silence, it will expand and connect to everything. Everything will speak to you. The trees, the mountains, the ocean and the sky will converse with you. Beast and birds, fish and reptiles and all the creeping and crawling creatures will talk to you. You will understand the language of silence as every sound will pull you into the void of nothingness.

Call the name of God with a passion that is irresistible until you realize that the caller is the one called. Chant until the chanted begins to chant itself within you. Then, your heart will echo with the Holy Name. This is the power of Self-resonance.[6] The cells of your body will take up the vibration of the primal sound and every hair will be tuned like violin strings to the Divine frequency. In the same manner that a wine glass is shattered into pieces when the glass particles begin to vibrate with the frequency of the sound of a singer, the mind is transcended when it resonates with the frequency of the holy name.

Susanna: Lord, we are conscious during the waking state but hardly are we in control of what happens in our dreams. How then can one remember God in this state?

The important thing is not the dream; the goal is to be aware of the dreamer. The dreamer is the screen. The dreams are as images projected on a screen. As long as the images are there, the screen is not evident. When the images disappear, the screen is witnessed as the unchanging reality. In the same way, you can only realize your Self as the dreamer, when the dreams are wiped away. The dream is the store of the subconscious mind. It is the record of your past deeds, thoughts, words and emotions and holds the imprint of all your impulses and tendencies, past desires and future predispositions. It is the seed of Adam's regeneration and preservation and the driving urge of Eve's passive and active tastes. The aim is to go beyond the subconscious mind.

Fall asleep with the sacred Word. When you fall asleep with the Name, you will divinize your dreams. This means that the vast data of the subconscious will be replaced with the Divine Name. Hence, you must sleep with the Name of God by injecting the primal sound into your subconscious mind. There is a little gap, which separates the waking and the sleeping states. It is that space between the waking and sleeping states when you are neither awake nor asleep. Few know about this interval which is the door to the unconscious Self (or the 'gate' to the Kingdom of God). If you auto-suggest the Name of God into this opening, the Divine word will weave its miracle even as you slumber.[7] You will become aware of that which neither sleeps nor wakes. If you seek to know where the 'I am' is, search for it within this gate. Only the saints have observed this phenomenon.

That which is conscious between the waking and sleeping states[8], between the inhalation and exhalation of breath, and between two consecutive thoughts is the 'I am' principle.

Thomas: Lord, does this mean calling your Name continuously until one falls asleep?

Do not be mechanical. When there is no love in what you do, that action is dead and is of no benefit. Love is the Spirit that animates every action. If you love God, you will always want to sleep with God like a baby in its mother's arms. Think of God as you fall asleep. Hug the Name in the cavity of your heart. This is like the hug of silence. It is a living closeness, which you feel with the reality of God even as you sleep. Although you may not see or touch the 'I am', you can feel the presence, and embrace it in your sleep. With practice, this awareness will become more concrete than the mattress on which your body rests.

Mary (the Divine Mother): Son, it may be possible to remember God while awake. In deep sleep, one is unconscious. How can one remember anything in the state of unconsciousness?

The deep sleep state (that is dreamless sleep) is characterized by two qualities: unawareness and rest. First, in deep sleep you are unaware of yourself. Not only are you unconscious of the Self but you are also unconscious of your unconsciousness. In deep sleep, everything is forgotten including the 'I' who forgot everything. This is why you come to know you have enjoyed deep sleep only after you have woken up from it.

Secondly, in deep sleep, you are completely at rest. The reason is simple. Rest is the absence of activity. The body-mind complex, which is responsible for activity is completely withdrawn in deep sleep and you remain in the state of 'I am'. The state of deep sleep is the state of silence. However, this state of silence happens to you unconsciously. The goal of life is to be in the state of rest in full awareness. When you realize the deep sleep state in full awareness, you are awake while asleep. When this happens, silence becomes one's natural state and the three states of the mind: waking, dreaming and sleeping become unified into one. The Self realized is fully conscious in each of the three states.

Thomas: Master, how can one be awake while asleep?

Watch your thoughts.

13

Watch Your Thoughts
...Be a Witness

Jesus said his disciples:
"Keep awake and watch."
Mark 14:38

Jesus went on a boat ride with his disciples to the other side of the lake. It happened that as they sailed, there came a storm of wind on the lake. The waves were breaking into the boat so that it was almost swamped. But Jesus was on the stern, his head on the cushion, asleep. The disciples woke him up saying, "Master, do you not care if we perish?" Jesus rebuked the wind saying, "Quiet now! Be calm." Immediately, the raging water ceased and there was great calm.[1]

The disciples said to one another, "Who is this man that even the winds obey him?"

Jesus said to them, "The wind of the mind is more ferocious than any raging storm. Truly, the mind is the wind turned inside and the secret of the wind is hidden in the mind. He who is able to calm the inner mind will control the external wind."

Peter: Lord, the flow of thoughts surge within me like the waves of an ocean, how is it possible to stop these waves?

When you identify with the waves, you will be tossed about like the waves. You are not the turbulent waves, you are the stillness, the deep ocean of the 'I am'. Watch your thoughts and do not identify with them. Just watch the waves as they rise and fall. Do not try to stop them, just observe. Thoughts lose their power of control when you watch. This is the sacred art of inner vigilance. The path to Self Knowledge requires constant inner vigilance of your thought patterns.

Watch yourself[2], that is, watch the one who is watching. Then you will discover that thoughts have no real existence. The Self alone is.

Peter: Lord, do teach us how we can consciously build a new thought energy pattern.

Why do you want to build new thought patterns? The mind is an obstacle to Self-awareness. The aim is to transcend thought. Think less until one thought (that is, the thought of God or 'I am') takes up your mental space. Then it is easy to go beyond thought. When you sow a particular thought in your mind and you think over it repeatedly, you increase the intensity of this thought pattern. Your mind has no particular shape but takes the shape of your thought. Your thought intensity depends on your power of concentration. When your thoughts are single and concentrated, your mind becomes one-pointed and integrated. To such an integrated single-minded one, nothing is impossible. Integrated thought makes your mind strong and only a strong mind can abide in the silence of the Self.

However, it is not just enough to build a strong mind. A strong mind is like a two edged-sword. It can cut in both ways - it can create and destroy. This is why you must build the power of thought with love. A mind saturated with love cannot entertain thoughts of violence. On the contrary, a strong mind without love is positively dangerous because of the tendency to use this mental strength for destructive purposes.

Therefore, you have three groups of individuals: persons whose minds are strong and saturated with love, persons who have strong minds but lack love, and weak-minded persons. A weak-minded person has an unsteady thought energy pattern. His mind is not steady with any particular thought shape but takes on the shape of so many changing thought patterns. Hence, the intensity of his thought energy field becomes very weak.

God is love. A strong mind is a mind with one-pointed thought. When this one-pointed thought is God, then your mental strength will be based on love. Let the object of your mental concentration be the thought of God, and then your mind will be filled with love. You can transcend the mind only with the power of love.

Thaddeus: Lord, so many worldly thoughts interfere with the thought of God.

A disciple came to his master and requested for a spiritual exercise. The master told him to think always of God. When he was on his way back, the master called him back and told him to be careful not to allow the form of a monkey to enter his mind. Before meeting the master the disciple never entertained the thought of a monkey. However, after the master told him not to think of monkeys, he was always thinking, "I should never allow a monkey to enter my mind". Thus, all the time, he was thinking of a monkey and he never thought of God. After a while he went back to the master and complained about his disturbing situation. The master told him, "I have asked you to think of God. What does the form of God mean? God is omnipresent and if you think of God, various things can come to your mind and there is nothing wrong. Even if a monkey comes to your mind, it simply means that God is omnipresent. See God in the monkey." Hence, seeing God in every form is the secret of raising every thought to the Divine frequency.

John: Lord, teach us the nature of thought. Why does it wield so much power?

Just as the moon reflects the light of the sun, thoughts are the reflections of the Self. On further investigation, you will discover that the moon has no light. In the same way, thoughts have no reality. The Self alone is and what you experience as the power of thought is only a reflection of Self-omnipotence.

However, the influence of thought is so great for those who live under the shadow of the moon 'light' (the world of thoughts). Thought is the energy equivalent of matter. Creation is solidified thought. The first quality of thought is its magnetic effect. Your thoughts are the most powerful magnetic force. They create an aura around your form, which build a magnetic energy field. You live and move within the magnetic energy field of your thought patterns. As you think, so you are!

The magnetic energy, which keeps the universe in motion, is

nothing but the thought of 'I am'. It is this magnetic power, which keeps the planets rotating and revolving around the sun and the sun around its own galaxy and the galaxies within the expanding universe. When you fill your mind with the thought of God, you align yourself to this universal magnetic force of the 'I am'.

As a magnetic force, your thoughts have positive and negative polarities. Everything that happens, or fails to happen to you have either been attracted or repelled by your magnetic thought energy field. You must therefore watch your thoughts because they will surely manifest in your life as reaction, reflection or resound.[1]

Whatever you experience in life is only the resound of your thought patterns. This whole world is only the reflection of your thought. What you see is but the expression of what you are. You are the seed, which gave rise to this cosmic tree. You create your world. In addition, whatever you do is only a reaction of your own thought patterns. As the thought, so is the action. As the action, so is the habit. As the habit, so is the character. Your character defines your destiny. Therefore, your destiny lies in your thought. Since your destiny is Divinity, you should fill your mind with the thought of God.

If you think, 'I am different from God', you separate yourself from yourself in self limitation. If you think, 'I am God', you realize the infinite potential of the 'I am'. As you think, so you are, so always think, 'I am God'. In this thought plane, the 'I am' emanates within itself all the attributes of God: Divine opulence, wealth, wellbeing, happiness, joy, fearlessness, wisdom, and so on.

Matthew: How is creation solidified thought?

Thought is the energy equivalent of matter and both are convertible.[3] Thought is like gaseous matter and matter is like solid thought. Mind is the dynamic side of matter. The rate of vibration makes you think that matter is different from thought. However, both are essentially one like the water molecules in the gaseous and solid states. Heat increases the rate of vibration and the rate of vibration determines the state. Thought is materialized when you reduce the 'temperature of thought' to the 'zero-thought-point' through the cooling agent of concentration. Concentration is the ability to hold on to the thought of God (awareness of God), for an uninterrupted period of time. This is the art of energy channeling or focusing. Energy is materialized only when it is channeled.

If you want to convert energy into mass, you have to hold just one thought for an uninterrupted period that corresponds to a time constant, which is the breaking point (materialization point) of thought. This constant is equal to 28.8 minutes.[4] This is the science of Divine Incarnation: "The Word became flesh."[5] or "Thought became Matter".

On the other hand, you can transfigure matter back to the state of pure thought, by raising its rate of vibration. The Prophet Elijah used this principle to transfigure his body into a 'chariot of fire'.[6]

Philip: Master, how can one hold just one thought for so long?

Through practice, you develop one-pointed attention. Your practice becomes easy and fast with the power of love. When you love something, it is easy for you to hold it in your mind for a long time. When you saturate the mind with the love of God, it becomes very easy for you to hold the thought of God through its breaking point. One who lacks love is bound to be weak-minded. When the mind expands in the form of countless thoughts, each thought becomes weak. However, as thoughts get resolved at a point the mind becomes strong and sharp. A person with such a strong mind abides in the Self.

Bartholomew: This means that we must always think of God with Love!

Love is the super glue and the centre that holds everything together. Love is the core of concentration. With love, you are able to hold the 'I am' thought through the breaking point of thought. With love, you will realize the Omega point where there is no thought vibration. No thought is the void of nothingness and the negation of nothingness[7] is silence. When one encounters silence, one's ability to materialize thoughts becomes instantaneous. What one wills, happens. When you say, 'Let there be', it is.[8] Through silence, one knows oneself as the 'isness' of everything that is. This is the destiny of being.

Thoughts have another great quality! They have a range or spectrum just like physical energy.[9] This range is determined by the rate of thought vibration or wavelength. Thoughts are like electromagnetic waves. They need no material medium for their transmission. Thus, light can travel through interplanetary and interstellar space from the sun and stars to the earth.

Your thoughts have the full spectrum of electromagnetic waves and much more. With the power of thought, you can do everything the scientist does with physical energy. The mind is more powerful than atomic energy, and mightier than the nuclear force. However, this entire mental energy is but a reflection of the 'I am' principle. As the light of the moon comes not from itself but from the sun, the energy of the mind is derived from the power of the 'I am'. Once you realize the 'I am', mental power becomes redundant.

The 'I am' is realized when the mind is able to abide in the 'Self' for an uninterrupted period. In this state, the mental wavelength is reduced to the 'zero omega point'. It is called the 'absolute vibration of thought'. Its rate is so fast it seems stationary. It is the meeting point of mind and spirit, sound and silence, action and inaction, being and non being. Beyond this point is the pathless path to Self knowledge.

14
The Pathless Path
...to Self Knowledge

Jesus said to them:
"You shall love the Lord your God... with all your soul"[1]
Mark 12:30

Andrew: Lord, teach us how to pray as John taught his disciples.[2]
Do not babble with many words when you pray, like those who are
ignorant, for the Father ('I am') knows what you need before you
ask.[3] Silence is the highest form of prayer. The prayer of silence is
the awareness that you are what you ask.[4] So you should pray like
this:

Our father, who 'I Am'
Hallowed is your Name
Your Kingdom is Within
For You are in me as 'I Am' in You
'I Am' the Bread of Life
'I Am' the Truth, the Awareness and the Bliss
'I Am' the Kingdom, the Power and the Glory, forever and ever, Amen.

Thomas: Lord, if we are what we ask, why pray?
The moment you are aware of yourself as that, you do not need to
pray. To whom shall you pray to since there is no one outside you?
Philip: Lord, you told the people to pray without ceasing?[5]
Pray to your Self. There is nothing outside.
*John: Lord, what does scripture mean when it says, "Thou shall love God
with your entire soul?"*
What is soul?
John: Soul is embodied Spirit.
What is Spirit?

John: God is Spirit.[6]

Therefore, Soul is God living in the body.

John: Your Words are Truth Lord.

This means loving God with all your Soul is, loving God with God. God is Spirit. Those who worship him must worship him in Spirit. This is to say; only the Spirit can know the Spirit. Only God can know God.[7]

John: Does the Spirit require any knowing process to know itself as Spirit?

In direct knowledge, the Spirit remains in the silence of itself, as 'I am that I am', full, absolute, eternal and infinite.

There is no effort to be, since you are already that. There is no need to want, since you are the fullness. There is no necessity to surrender, since there is no other than you. There is no volition to attain that, which you have always been. There is no urge to move, since there is no place you are not. To remain, as the 'I am that I am' is direct knowledge. To be as you are, is the pathless path to Self-realization.

John: But my mind is always standing in between my Self and me?

How many are you?

John: There seems to be two personalities warring within me!

Actually, there are three: the one you think you are (the body), the one others think you are (the mind), and the one you truly are (the Self).[8] The Self is the Reality. The Mind is the Mirror. The body is the reflected object. When the mirror of the mind is removed the body image will also disappear. What remains is the Reality, your true Self.

John: How do I remove this mirror?

Be still. Be yourself. Practice 'being', that is, live in the awareness that there is nothing to be. Live as if you are God. Then remove the 'if' because you are that.

John: But my mind is always taking me away from this stillness!

The mind is like the balloon. The air inside is limited love. The air outside is universal love. When you fill the balloon of the mind with more love, it will burst and the air inside will merge with the air outside. You will move from limited love to universal love, from soul to Spirit, and from 'I am this or that' to 'I am that I am'. Expand the infinite boundaries of the Self. That is another way to deal with the mind – Love.

The heart is love. The head is 'thought'. Sink your head into the heart. That is, fill the mind with love. God is love, live in love.[9] When the mind is in the heart, the mind does not exist as such. It is like what happens when sound encounters silence. It disappears. Mind is sound. Heart is silence. The Self can be realized only in the heart.[10]

Philip: Why is it impossible for the mind to comprehend God?

Who can comprehend 'that' which has no end or understand 'that', which has no stand? The Self is beyond the mind. To realize the Self, one has to relinquish this imperative to understand and the need to comprehend. One must enter into the 'cloud of unknowing' by stripping the mind of the desire to know.

Imagine a child seeking to transfer the waters of the ocean into a tiny cup in his hand.[11] It is like one trying to measure 'that' which has no dimensions.

Those who seek the knowledge of the 'I am' do not try to solve the mystery. Spiritual truths are not solved rather they are lived. You are the 'I am' which is the mystery without beginning or end.

Matthew: How could there be knowledge, if there is no knower who is separate from the known?

Self knowledge is the awareness of oneness. Since there is only one, where is the second to be known? Self-realization is beyond the knower, the known and the knowing process. It is simply 'Awareness'. That is why you do not need to do anything in order to know it. You are that already – the One. All that is required is to be still. There cannot be anything simpler. The mind complicates the simple.

Andrew: Lord, how can one cope with the day-to-day worldly activities without the mind?

Immediately you realize the 'Self', you do not need the mind to cope with the world because you will not see the world apart from the 'Self'. You will know your Self as the creator and the created. You will not need a particular eye to see because you will see with every eye. You will not need a particular ear to hear because you will hear with every ear. In addition, you will not need legs to go to places because everywhere is in you. More so, you can see without the eye, hear without the ear, and be without the legs!

When the sun has risen, do you need the reflected light of the moon to see? In the same way, when the sun of the universal 'I am' resurrects within you, the reflected light of the mind becomes redundant. Yes, the mind is indispensable as long as one is not aware of the 'I am'. As long as the mind persists, the world is perceived as a separate entity. Since the mind creates the worlds, you will need the mind to sustain the worlds. Once the mind is not there, the question of how to cope with the world will disappear because there is no world without the mind.

For example, the things you see and experience during the day exist only because the mind is awake. Also during the night when you are dreaming, your dream world is real as long as the mind is active. However, when the mind is withdrawn during the deep sleep state, or in a faint, or in the silence of meditation, there is no world and there are no activities.

James: Lord, we have been able to understand all you taught us with the help of our minds. If there is no mind, how can we understand you?

If there is no mind, there will be no need for the teaching. However, because your mind still persists, one mind is telling the other, 'drop the mind'. The moment you decide to abide in the stillness, you must do away with everything I have taught you. No one can enter the stream of truth with the garment of the mind.[12]

Thaddeus: It is a fact that the wonders of the world have been created by the mind.

The real wonder is the Self. Only the Self-realized can generate real wonders. The mind makes you think that its powers are original to it and you cannot realize this mistake until you remove the mind. This is the deluding power of the mind. It creates the impression that the Self is not real whereas the Self is the only reality. On the other hand, it makes you think that the world is out there, independent and existing of itself whereas the world is only a reflection of the 'I am'. In this way, the mind makes the image look like the reality and makes you confuse the image as the reality.

Simon: How can I live without thoughts?

You have been so accustomed to "thinking" that you think you are because you think.[13] However, this is not the case. Thinking is not your real nature. In fact, the more you think, the more you move away from your 'Christ' essence which is the 'I am' within you. The more you think, the more you separate yourself from yourself as reflections of yourself. You are pure existence. Your true Self is the state of no thought. Thoughts are mental noise. When there is so much noise within you, how can you be aware of the stillness? The moment your mind is still, you will know the 'I am'.

15

Be Still and Know
... That 'I am' God

Jesus said to them:
"Seek first the kingdom of God and every other thing will be added
unto you."
Luke 12:31

A young man ran up and knelt at the feet of Jesus and asked him, "Good Master, what must I do to inherit eternal life?" Jesus said to him, "Go sell all you have, give the money to the poor, come and follow me." On hearing this, the man went away very sad because he was a man of great wealth.[1]

Jesus looked round and said to his disciples, "How hard it is for one who has identified the Self with objects to enter the Kingdom of God. It is easier for a Camel to pass through the eye of a needle than for one with identifications (that is, the sense of 'I am this or that') to enter the kingdom of God."[2]

Peter: Lord, we have left everything and followed you. What shall be our reward?[3]

If you have truly left everything, you will not seek for rewards. However, because you do, your identifications still remain. In truth, everything is given only when you give up this sense that you are giving anything. Give up this sense of separation. Since the Self alone is, who is the second to give? You are the Self which holds within itself the gift, the giver and the given.

Philip: Lord what then must we do to enter the Kingdom?

There is no need to do anything to be that which you are already. The Self is the Kingdom of God. Since the Self is all there is, there can be no within or without because there is nothing outside the Self. For those who are still caught in the illusion of duality, we speak of 'entering', 'realising', 'attaining', 'loving' and so on. However, these concepts do not express the truth of the 'I am'. Be still and know that 'I am'. In stillness, there is no movement because you are beyond space and time. In stillness the whole of creation can pass through the eye of a needle since the Self is the smallest of the small and the biggest of the big.[4]

For those who have identified the Self with objects ('I am this or that') it is impossible to know the Self as 'I am that I am'. You cannot experience both at the same time.[5]

Thomas: Why do you tell the people one thing and tell us another?

To you is granted the secret of the Knowledge of God but to those who are outside (that is, who live in duality) everything comes in parables.[6] So that they hear, but they will never understand because they live in the mind.[7] The mind wants 'something' to do and cannot abide in that stillness which is beyond effort. Therefore, for those who still live in the shadow of thought, we speak about effort until it is realized that no effort is needed. This realization happens spontaneously. At last, after a long journey in quest of the Kingdom, you find out that you have only moved from your Self to your Self.

In the initiation into the inner mystery of our ancient Cabbala, the neophyte is led through different levels of spiritual awareness. At the last stage, he is told, "You are the one you are searching for." He has to pass through rigorous levels of spiritual discipline in order to realize that the seeker is the one sought.

Thomas: Without effort, how can anything happen?

Stillness is not inactivity. Stillness is the absence of the 'I' concept. When you are serving without the ego, you are still. When eating without the ego, you are still. When you are speaking without the ego, you are silent. When the ego is absent, although you are acting, yet you are at rest.

For example, what do you do in order for the earth to rotate, for the sun to shine or the tree to grow? It just happens. The circulatory, digestive, respiratory, elimination and nervous processes of your body happen spontaneously. In being, that is, this awareness that there is nothing to become, everything just happens. Stillness is the being of every activity.

Be in that awareness where there is nothing to cling to, nothing to do, and nothing to become. Be still.

Philip: Lord, our problem is how to abide in this stillness. The mind seems to be a major obstacle.

Your mind wants to cling to something. It behaves as the worm, which cannot let go of a leaf unless it holds unto another. Understand the nature of the mind then it is easy to let go. It has no reality apart from the Self. You are that 'Self' and the mind cannot operate if you do not give it authority to do so. Since you are the one who gave the mind the power to rule you, all you have to do is to withdraw these powers from the mind by being a witness. You give authority to the mind when you 'try to' engage in thought and when you 'try to' disengage with thought. 'Trying to think' is effort and 'trying not to think' is effortlessness. You are a witness when you go beyond these two. The moment you are a witness, the mind will cease to trouble you.

To be a witness is to watch. The art of watching presupposes that you are unaffected, unattached and not involved. This means that when you watch, you do not judge, analyze, interpret, describe, condemn, or commend. You just witness. There is a vacuum created in the art of watching. Suddenly, you are not there. The mind is not there. Everything disappears into the nothingness including the idea that one is a witness. There is an awesome awareness of the oneness of being.

The root of thought is the 'I' thought or the ego. Without it, no thought is possible because it creates other thoughts. You are able to go beyond thought just by watching the root. The moment you watch the 'I' thought, you remain in the 'I-I' or 'I am I' state of silence. Whenever a thought arises in your mind, enquire into the origin of that thought. Ask yourself, 'to whom do these thoughts arise?'[7] The answer is 'I'. Then enquire, 'who am I?' and know that this question has no answer. That is to say, "be still and know that 'I am'."

Part V:
Creation

Jesus said to them:
'The truth is, before Abraham ever was, I am'
John 8:57

If the 'I am' alone is, truly nothing is created, since nothing is
added to the 'I am', before, during and after the creative process,
and because nothing is removed, nothing is dissolved.

16
Before Time Began
...No-thing is Created

*"In the beginning was the word and the word was with God and the
word was God."*
John 1:1

Jesus said to those following him, "You will come to know the Truth
and the truth will set you free. Whoever keeps my word will never
see death."[1]

*Barnabas (one of the scribes): Abraham is dead and the prophets are dead,
and yet you say, "Whoever keeps my word will never know the taste of
death." Are you greater than our father Abraham, who is dead?*

Your father Abraham rejoiced to think he would see my day; he saw
it and was glad.[2]

Barnabas: You are not fifty yet and you have seen Abraham!

In truth I tell you, before Abraham ever was, I am.[3]

When he said this, some people in the crowd picked up stones
to throw at him. Jesus withdrew from them and went to a lonely
place with his disciples. There the disciples raised up the question
concerning his claim of pre-existence.

*Matthew: Lord, we did not understand you when you said that Abraham
saw your day and that you existed before him.*

Before time was born, 'I am'. Then a primal urge arose within me to
separate myself from myself so that I could love myself. Thus, the
One became three and the three became five and the five became
many.[4] However, the many is the One, there is no second. 'I am' the
One who is beyond time, without beginning and without end. 'I am'
the three who is the holy trinity: Father, Son and Holy Ghost; the
three creative powers: thought, word and deed; the three categories
of time: past, present and future; and the three states of the mind:

waking, dreaming and sleeping. 'I am' the five, which are the five elements, space, air, fire, water and earth. 'I am' the many which is the multiplicity and variety you find in creation. Just as the human body is a combination of the five elements, everything you find in the cosmos is an amalgamation of the five elements in varying proportions. The five is the one, which has multiplied itself into the many. The seed gave rise to the tree. From this tree came many seeds, which gave rise to the forest. However, this forest with so many trees has come from a single seed. It has always been the 'I am', who has separated itself from itself in order to love itself.

The 'I am' is timeless. Before creation, there was none outside it to say what it was. You could not say it was 'being', 'non-being', 'light', or 'darkness'. If you said, it was truth, who was there to know it? If you said it was silence, who was the witness? In addition, if you said, it was love, who was the beloved?

The primal urge that arose in the 'I am' to re-create itself in order to love itself is the root 'I' thought through which the Self reflected upon itself as images of itself. This reflection is the light of love. Where there is love, there is light and where there is light, there is life. Live in the light of love. With the light of love, you are aware of the Self in all. Expand your heart into universal love. Love all. Love until you see all as the reflection of yourself. Then you will know creation as your own recreation.

The whole of creation is born and sustained in love. Love is life. To live is to dance and to dance is to celebrate. Celebrate love in the dance of life. The whole universe is dancing, the moon around the earth, the earth around the sun, the sun around its galaxy, and the galaxies around the boundless space of the ever-expanding universe. It is love that makes the male dance around the female, the female around her young, the young around the old, the old around the dead and the dead around the living in the infinite circle of life. Again, in love, the second dances around the minute, the minute around the hour, the hour around the day, the day around the month, the month around the year, and the year around the ages in the eternal wheel of time. The 'I am' is the center of this dance, its beat and its dance steps. Creation is the dance of the Self.

From the Self, all have evolved
Through the Self, all are revolving
Within the Self, all will dissolve
Therefore, nothing is evolved
Nothing is revolving
And nothing is dissolved
Since the Self alone is.

What you perceive as creation is like the movement of the tortoise in and out of its own shell. In both processes nothing is added or removed from the unity of the tortoise. This is true of the Self. The sense of movement makes you think that something new is being created, but it has always been the Self.

Peter: Lord, does the Self need to create itself in order to know itself?

In the beginning, the 'I am' reflected upon itself in order to know itself, and this is how the 'I am' became light[5] – through its own reflection. Just as you can see the sun only through the rays of the sun, you are aware of the Self only through the light of the Self. Just as you can see your eye only through the reflection in the mirror, the 'I am' can see itself only through the mirror of the mind.

The 'I am' is beyond sound. Before creation, there was no sound because there was no second to hear it. Then the 'I am' re-sounded itself within itself in order to commune with itself. Creation therefore is only the resound of Silence. The whole cosmos is composed of the primal sound of 'I am' emerging from the womb of silence. Everything is one continuum of radiation, vibration and materialization. The Radiation of the 'I am' (silence) gave birth to the vibration of thought (sound) and through this vibration; the whole of creation (matter) came into existence. Spirit, mind and matter are inseparable.

Reality is an ocean of silence and what you see at the surface, namely the waves of the visible universe, is only the resound of 'I am'. At the depth of reality is sublime stillness. When you find that gap between the rising and fading of sound, you will know that silence (no-thing-ness) is the root of everything. In truth, no-thing is created, since no-thing can be added to the One and no-thing can be removed from the One. This is the wisdom of Qoheleth who said, "There is One alone and there is not a second. Yes, he has neither child nor brother: yet there is no end to all his labor."[6]

17
The Universe is My Body
...The Life Stream, My Blood

Jesus said to his disciples:
"Take and eat. This is My Body"
Luke 26:26

Jesus crossed the Sea of Galilee and a large crowd followed him. When it was evening, his disciples asked him to dismiss the crowd so that they could go to the villages and buy some food for themselves. But Jesus, filled with compassion, instructed them to make the crowd sit down on the ground. He took seven loaves and after giving thanks he broke them and began handing them to his disciples who gave them to the crowds. They all ate as much as they wanted, men, women and children that numbered more than five thousand.[1]

Next day, Jesus and his disciples made their way to Capernaum. The crowd came looking for him. When they found him, they said, "Master, when did you come here?" Jesus replied, "The truth is that you are looking for me not because you believed in me but because you had all the bread you wanted to eat. Do not work for bread that goes bad but work for food that endures for eternal life which I will give you."[2]

Nicodemus: "Sir, give us that bread always."

"I am the bread of life. Anyone who eats this bread will live for ever. And the bread that I shall give is my flesh, for the life of the world."[3]

Hearing this, the people were disturbed.

Barabbas: "This is intolerable language. How can you give us your flesh to eat?"

If you do not eat my flesh, and drink my blood, you have no life in you, for my flesh is real food and my blood is real drink. Whoever eats my flesh and drinks my blood lives in me and I live in that person.[4]

After this, many of his disciples went away and stopped following him.[5] At supper, while he was eating with the twelve, Jesus took bread, and when he had said the blessing he broke it and gave it to them. 'Take it and eat', he said, 'this is my body'. Then he took a cup and when he had given thanks he handed it to them and all drank from it and he said to them, 'this is my blood.'" [6]

John: Lord, how is the bread your body and the wine, your blood?

When I said that the bread was my flesh and the wine, my blood, I meant that all life forms, with flesh and blood, are to be regarded as 'Christ'.[7] The whole universe is the body of 'Christ' and the life stream that flows in its veins is the blood of 'Christ'. There is only one body, the body of 'Christ', which is the 'I am' Principle.[8]

Whenever you sit at the table, remember that 'I am' the life principle in the food you eat. 'I am' also the fire principle that digests the food in your body and 'I am' the soul principle, which dwells in the temple of the body.

The body consists of the food you eat. 'I am' the Bread of Life'.[9] 'I am' the Life in all. When you consciously receive the 'Christ' in the communion of the eternal presence, know that you are what you receive, the 'I am' consciousness.

The entire universe is sustained by this principle of give and take. It is in giving that you receive and in dying that you are born again into the newness of life.[10] Without this exchange of 'Holy Communion', the whole cosmos would collapse as the life of the cosmos consists of this metabolism. It is the cosmic conversion of matter into energy and energy back into matter.

Judas: Lord, how is the universe your body?

You cannot comprehend the vastness of the body of 'Christ' with your limited mind. When you think you are an individual body, you limit the 'I am' to the functions of the human brain. How then can you grasp the vastness of the 'I am' or 'Christ' (Cosmic) Consciousness?

When you look at the earth, you will realize how infinitesimal it is in relation to the solar system in which it is situated.[11] The solar system itself is also microscopic in relation to the galaxy which harbours it, and this galaxy is but one of billions of galaxies in the ever-expanding universe.[12] In this picture, it is almost impossible to situate the physical body. Yet this big inconceivable physical universe is like a speck in the body of 'Christ'. You will now understand how you limit the limitless 'I am' when you identify with the physical body.

The 'I am' is the heartbeat of creation and just as you can move any part of your physical body from one place to another with the power of your will, so also the 'I am' is responsible for the movement and operations of the universes. Because your body is within the body of 'Christ', what you often refer to as your individual will is nothing but the will of the 'I am'. You are moving within the freedom of the Self which itself is beyond freedom.

The body of 'Christ' is more than you know. This gross physical universe, visible and invisible, which looks so big and inconceivable, is only a tiny cell within the subtle astral body of 'Christ', the universe of thought vibrations. This world corresponds to the dream state. Again, the subtle mental universe is like an atom within the causal universe, which is the sphere of limitless light, and relates to the deep sleep state. The physical is like a cell within the mental and the mental is like an atom within the causal.[13] These three worlds, gross, subtle and causal, are within 'Christ'. In 'Christ' they move and live and have there being.

Since your true Self is the 'Christ', the three universes are within you! The entire cosmos, gross, subtle and causal is contained in your 'I am'. Yet, the 'I am' is beyond the three bodies. When you identify the 'I am' with the body, you worry about little things, whether you have enough food, drink and clothes. How trivial are the things that upset you. You are angry, depressed, envious, and jealous about insignificant details which steal away your peace and happiness. The comforts and cares of the body take up all your time and thought. However, you are more than food and clothing.[14] You are more than the body! Once you concern yourself about the real purpose for which you are born – namely the knowledge of the 'I am' – the universe will provide all your bodily needs without the asking.[15]

Mary: Lord, we are only aware of the physical body in the material universe and not the other dimensions.

You have three eyes: the physical eyes, the mental eye and the spiritual eye. You are able to see the physical world with the aid of the physical eyes. These eyes are active during the waking state and can only see what is in front of them and external characteristics of objects like colors, shapes, appearances and dimensions.

The mental eye is operative during the dreaming state. When you are dreaming, your physical eyes are closed but you see another world all together which are as real to you as long as your dream lasts. You see cities, stars, the sun and moon, seas and oceans, peoples and trees. You see this entirely new world with the mental eyes. This is the eye of imagination. It is more penetrative than the physical eye because it sees the inner meaning and purpose of a thing. The mental eye can see even when the physical eyes are closed or damaged. This is why the blind person can say, 'I see what you mean!' It is mental insight.

Although the mental can see without the physical, the latter cannot see without the former. When the mental eye is closed, the physical eye cannot see. Hence, the physical depends totally on the mental. For example, when the mind is absent, although the physical eyes may be wide open, they cannot see a thing. Somebody might be right in front of you but you fail to see him because your mind is not there. Therefore, one may cope in the physical world without the physical eye but it is impossible to cope in the physical world without the mental eye. Hence, the physical depends on the mental.

The spiritual eye is the eye of the 'I'. It is also called the third eye or the single eye. 'When your eye is single, your whole body will be filled with light.'[16] This is the limitless light of the 'I am' effulgence. The third eye is open when you go beyond the body-mind complex. That is, when you are able to close the mental and physical eyes. Again, just as the physical eye is inoperative without the mental, the mental is useless without the spiritual. Moreover, the spiritual eye can see without the mental and physical eyes.

The spiritual eye is 'I-Sight' or 'One-sight'. It perceives the truth of everything from within. It is the power of intuitive awareness. When the third eye is open, one is aware of the 'One in the many', the 'Divinity in humanity', the 'Spirit in matter', the 'Creator in the created', and the 'Silence in the sound'. The three categories of time, past, present and future disappear in the 'now'.

The third eye is the eye of the 'I am'. The scriptures declare that, 'The eye of Yahweh (that is, 'I am') is everywhere'.[17] Where shall one go to escape from the 'I am'? Where shall one flee from its presence? If you go down to the place of the dead, the 'I am' is there. If you speed away on the wings of the dawn, and dwell beyond the ocean, even there the hand of the 'I am' will be guiding you. If you say, "Let the darkness cover me, and the night wrap itself around me," even darkness is not dark for the 'I am' and before it, the night is as clear as the day. The 'I am' knows you through and through and your being holds no secret from it.[18] Those whose third eye is open abide in the causal dimension of Limitless Light.

Thomas: Lord, how is the Self beyond freedom?

If God alone is, the idea of freedom is inconceivable. The concept of freedom applies as long as you think there is something separate from God. But since God is the one and only, where is the second to choose from? For example, you can decide to move your body from here to there. Hence, you conclude you have freedom of movement. However, if God is everywhere, you cannot say he is free to move from here to there because he is both here and there simultaneously.

Thomas: But God created us in freedom.

Creation is the recreation of God. What is, has always been and what will be, is what has been. There is nothing new.[19] It has always been God (the one) separating himself from himself in order to recreate himself. In this process, nothing is ever added to the one and nothing is removed.

God's omnipresence means that God alone is. He is the presence of all that is present and he is fully present in his omnipresence. That is, God's presence is continuous, full and integrated. God is not more present in some places, planes or things than he is in others. For example, God is not more present in heaven than he is on earth. Hence, if God is fully above as he is below, then he is continuously full in His omnipresence – in heaven as on earth, in man as in beast, within as without. God is the fullness and what you see as creation is the fullness taken from God's fullness which is the same undivided fullness. There is nothing outside God.

Philip: Lord, is God fully present in the stone as he is in humans?

God's presence cannot be partial presence or else he will be divided in himself. It is either God is in the stone or he is not there. If he is in the stone, then he must be fully present in the stone. If he is not in the stone, then he is fully absent in it. However, if God is absent in some objects, then, he is not omnipresent. On the other hand, if you believe that God is omnipresent, then he must be fully present in the stone.

Philip: Is the stone God?

The stone is unaware of itself as God. Man as the crown of creation has evolved the ability to know himself as God. Once you become aware of the Self, you will realize God's full presence in everything. The whole of creation is groaning for the birth of this knowledge.[20]

Mary: Why is God's presence felt more in some places than others?

This is because you have been conditioned to believe that God is more present in some places or things than in others. So you feel him more when you go to these places or come into contact with these objects. For example, you believe that God dwells in the ark of the covenant kept in the sanctum of the Temple. But in truth, God is not more present in those tablets of stone kept in the ark[21] than he is in other stones.

Mary: Lord, it is hard to see God in everything.

The 'I am' is fully present in the smallest of the small and in the biggest of the big. If a thing exists, it exists in God's existence. If a thing is consciousness, it is conscious in God's consciousness. God alone is and anything that is, in so far as it is, is in the *isness* of God. This *isness* is the 'I Amness' in all. In God we all live and move and have our being and there is nothing apart.[22]

There is no space or cell or atom that is not fully occupied by the 'I am'. Every part of you is fully filled with the 'I am' consciousness. Every space within your body, every thought within your mind, and every soul within your spirit is completely pervaded by this 'I Amness'. Hence, God is totally within you as you are within him.

If God is fully present within and outside of you, that is, if there is no presence within you that is not God's presence, then, you cannot be separate from God. If God is omnipresent, this means you are God.

18

God from God
...Begotten, Not Made.

Jesus said to them:
"Is it not written in your own law that God said,
'You are Gods'?"
John 10:34

Jesus was in the Temple walking up and down the Portico of Solomon. It was the Feast of Dedication in Jerusalem. Someone among the crowd asked him, "Are you the Christ?"[1]

Jesus replied, "The Father and I are one."[2]

Hearing this, some of the people picked up stones to throw at him.

Jesus said to them, "I have shown many good works from my Father; for which of these are you stoning me?"

"We are stoning you not for doing a good work", they replied, "but for blasphemy; though you are only a man, you claim to be God."[3]

Jesus answered, "Is it not written in your law:[4] I said, you are Gods. So it uses the word "Gods" of those people to whom the word of God was addressed – and scripture cannot be false. Why then do you say, "You are blaspheming" because I said, "I am God."[5] Truly, I am God and you too are God."

Barabbas: How many gods are there if everyone is god?

Can you count the drops that make up the ocean? Yet, the ocean is one. There is only one God. He lives in all as the 'I am'. The 'I am' in you is not different from the 'I am' in all. If the 'I am' is one, then there is only one God manifesting through different forms.

Barabbas: God is infinite but we are finite.

A finite being cannot come from infinity. If you are a child of infinity, then you are infinite. If you are separate from God, it means you exist outside existence. This is a contradiction in terms.

Simeon: Why do you refer to your Self as the "only son of God"?

All are God. In God, there are no first born and no last born, for God is Spirit and that which comes from Spirit is eternal. That which is eternal has no beginning and it has no end. It has no first and it has no last because it is beyond time and spatial separation. In God, nothing is created because nothing can exist outside God. God is the fullness, the perfection, the absolute, to which nothing can be added or removed. You, as the 'I am' are that fullness, who has always been and will always be – the fullness. In stillness, God is like the tortoise within its own Self. In creation, the Self projects itself outside itself. In this Self-projection, it has always been the Self. Truly, nothing new[6] has been created. The sense of movement makes you think that something is being created.

The creative 'word' of God is God.[7] It is the primal sound of silence, the root 'I' thought (or sound). The 'I' thought is in everyone as the first and only begotten Son of God. It is the first seed of all that is, the first born of all creation.[8] Without this I-thought, there is no creation. It is the seed, which has given rise to the 'Tree of Life'. It is also the only seed of all that is, since all other seeds have come from the variations of this primal seed. It is the origin of time and the beginning of creation. It is also the middle and the end, the inside and the outside of every manifestation. Just as sound is not separate from the silence, the word is not different from God.

"In the beginning was the word and the word was with God and the word was God."[9]

> *"All things were made and came into existence through it*
> *And without it was not one thing made*
> *That has come into being."*[10]

Different religions refer to this primal sound of silence by different names. The Mandukya Upanishad of the Sanathana Dharma (the most ancient Hindu scriptures), says:

"Aum, the 'word' is all this, the whole universe
All that is past, present and future is indeed Aum
And whatever else there is, beyond the threefold division of time
That too is Aum." [11]

Every atom in the cosmos is a resound of the primal sound known as 'I', 'Aum', 'Amen', or simply, the 'Word'. The heart of creation beats with this primal sound. When you are aware of this sound, you are one with the music of being and becoming; one with the all-pervading sound stream, which is dimensionless. You are one with the 'Word' of God and like the mystics, you will begin to hear the echo of the divine 'Word' in the sky, the earth, the moon and the entire universe and you will know that you as the 'Christ Consciousness' are indeed the only 'Son of God'.

Part VI:
The 'Cross'

Jesus said to them:
*"Unless a grain of wheat falls into the earth and dies, it remains a single
grain; but if it dies it yields a rich harvest"* [1]
John 12:25

Unless you die, you will not live!
For the Christ is the 'I-less I am'.

19

Playing Death
...The Sermon on the Mount

Jesus said to them:
'Whoever seeks to save his life will lose it, and whoever loses his life will preserve it.'
Luke 17:33

Seeing the multitudes, Jesus went up to a mountain and when he was seated, his disciples came to him. Filled with compassion, he opened his mouth and taught them saying:

> *Blessed are the poor in spirit: for theirs is the kingdom of heaven.*
> *Blessed are they that mourn: for they shall be comforted.*
> *Blessed are the meek: for they shall inherit the earth.*
> *Blessed are those who hunger and thirst for righteousness: for they*
> *   shall be filled.*
> *Blessed are the merciful: for they shall obtain mercy.*
> *Blessed are the pure in heart: for they shall see God.*
> *Blessed are the peacemakers: for they shall be called the children of*
> *   God.*
> *Blessed are those who are persecuted for righteousness' sake: for theirs*
> *   is the kingdom of heaven.*[1]

Whoever seeks to save his life will lose it, and whoever loses his life will preserve it.

Once, a certain king decided to give up his kingdom and all worldly things and become the disciple of a spiritual master. During the time of probation, the master put him to test. He was to sweep up the garbage in the monastery everyday and take this out of the village.

The other disciples pleaded with the master to relieve him of this duty since he was used to the comforts of the kingdom. The master knowing the aim he had in mind said, "We shall have a test."

One day, while he was taking his garbage pail out of the village, someone knocked against him and all the garbage were spilled on the ground. The disciple-king looked back and said to the person, "Well, thank your stars. It is not the days past. What can I tell you?" When this news was brought to the master, he said, "Did I not tell you that the time has not yet come?"

After some time, a test was made again. This time, the king-disciple looked at the man who had knocked against him and said nothing. Again, this was reported to the master who said, "Did I not tell you that the time has not yet come?"

After a long period, he was tested again the third time. This time he did not look at the man who spilled his basket. He took all that was there in the basket and carried it along. When this was narrated to the master, he said, "Now is the time, now he can play death."[2]

When you play death, you are dead to all the wrong things that come to you but you are alive to every good thing that can go from you.

Peter: Lord, explain to us the meaning of your sermon on the mount. What is 'poverty of Spirit'?
When the 'I am' is stripped of the sense of 'me' and 'mine', the Self is aware of itself as God. They lack nothing those who are poor in Spirit. Theirs is the kingdom and there is nothing outside.

Secondly, the process of stripping the 'I am' of the garments of 'me' and 'mine' brings about 'mourning'. Hence, they shall be comforted, those who pass through this purification.

Blessed are the meek. The meek are the humble. The humble are those who have no 'I' concept.

"Blessed are those who hunger and thirst for righteousness. Only the Self is right because there is nothing left. Where there is righteousness, there is Truth and where there is Truth, there is God.

The Self is the embodiment of Truth. Hence, those who hunger and thirst for righteousness, shall be filled with the Truth of the Self.

Be merciful unto yourself. When you condemn 'others' you condemn yourself since you are what you see and you see what you are. There is no 'other' apart from the 'I am'.

And truly blessed are the pure in heart, they are one with God. The heart is the seat of the Self. God lives in the heart. When the Self is alone as 'I am that I am', the heart shines in its pristine purity.

Thomas: Lord, has this heart anything to do with the physical body?
The heart is not any physiological organ. It is neither inside nor outside the body. There can be no in or out for it since it alone exists. The heart is another name for Self, Silence, 'I am', God or Love. However, as long as you identify yourself with the body, the heart is where the ego rises and merges back.[10] This is the seat of your Spiritual Self located few inches to the right of your chest. This is the meaning of the Scripture which says, "A wise man's heart is at his right hand; but the fool thinks it is at his left."[4] Whenever anyone says, 'myself' or 'I', they point to this place. This is the experience of all, irrespective of age, culture or country. Even a little child will point to this centre while referring to the 'Self' principle.

Blessed are the peacemakers: for they shall be called the children of God. Peace is the bliss of being. Being is that awareness where there is nothing to become. When the Self remains in itself as the Self, it is being. This is the 'I am' peace.[5] It is complete joy.[6] When the Self projects itself as 'this' or 'that' it is becoming. This is worldly agitations. The presence of those who abide in the peace of the Self instils peace in the heart of all.

Blessed are those who are persecuted for righteousness' sake: for theirs is the kingdom of heaven. You are blessed when you do everything for the sake of the Self. The seekers of the Self are non-violent. They act from the inspiration of the 'I am'. They never react to the agitations of the world (the mind). Established in the stillness of the Self, they are equal in praise and in blame, gain and loss, success and failure, rich and poor, hot and cold.

This is why I say to you: Love your enemies[7], because there are none. Give away everything you have (this sense of 'me' and 'mine') and you will be perfect, lacking nothing.[8] When someone slaps you on one cheek, turn the 'other'[9] since there is no other. When someone tells you, 'walk one mile with me', go two[10] since there is no place you are not. If something is taken away from you, do not try to get it back[11] since there is nothing that is not yours. Do not expect any return from your good deeds[12] since there is no one to give it anyway. If someone asks for your coat, give him your shirt as well[13] since your true Self is naked.[14] Do not judge and you will not be judged since you condemn yourself when you judge.[15] The measure you give is the measure you receive since you are both.[16] Be alike to everyone since there is only one.[17] If you want to be the greatest, be the least[16] since you are equally both. If you want to gain life, then you must first die[18] since the Self remains unaffected. Be in the world like the lotus born and bred in the mud but unaffected by the slush.[19] Yes! Come to me and learn the secret of death which is the Way of the Cross.

20
The Way of the Cross
...The Negation of the Ego

Jesus said to them:
"If any of you wants to be my disciple, you must put aside your selfish ambition, shoulder your cross daily, and follow me."
Luke 9:23

Gethsemane is an even plot of ground lying between the foot of Mount Olives and the brook of Kidron. It is well-planted with olive trees and evoked a beauty which made people think it was the original Garden of Eden. Jesus left with Peter, James and John and entered into this garden as was his custom.[1] He knew the time had come to restore the ancient but living tradition of the Tree of Knowledge.[2] Here he began to teach his close disciples the Path of the Cross which is the Negative Way through which one is lifted up on the Tree of Knowledge.

Jesus said to them, "Anyone who comes to me without hating (that is, non identification with) father, mother, wife, children, brothers, sisters, yes and his own life too, cannot be my disciple. If any of you wants to be my disciple, you must renounce yourself, take up your cross and follow me."[3]

Peter: Lord, what is the meaning of the 'Cross'?

The 'Cross' is the annihilation of the 'I' concept which is the root of all concepts. It is the essence of the 'Christ' or the 'I am' principle and the quintessence of all religions. When the ego is crucified, the 'Christ' which is the immortal Spirit will resurrect. Unless you die, you will not live. Unless you negate the 'I', you cannot realize the 'I am'.

Peter: How to deal with the ego?

The ego is the shadow of the Self. Hence, trying to deal with the ego is like someone chasing his own shadow or like the thief trying to catch the thief which he is. When you seek the root of the ego, you will discover it has no existence. Imagine a dog barking at its own image at the mirror! It thinks there are two dogs whereas there is only one. The image is real as long as you think there is 'another' separate from you. However, that 'other' is only a projection of the Self on the screen of the Self. The ego is a false sense of separation because nothing is separate.

James: Are suffering and death necessary for the realization of the Self?

Why should you suffer to know that which you are already and why should you die in order to know you are deathless? The Cross is not a symbol of suffering and death. Rather, the Cross teaches you how not to suffer by destroying the root of suffering and how to go beyond death by annihilating the very seed of birth. The ego, this false sense of separateness, is the root of suffering and death. The ego is the ignorance of the Self (that the Self alone is).[4] It is the ego that says, 'I am not God'. Its counterpart is humility. The humble acknowledge their oneness with God. The proud feel they are separate.[5]

James: Lord, the world cannot exist without the ego yet you say, "The ego has no existence."

Like a mirage in the desert, the ego is a phantom of the Self. Suppose you fall asleep and in a terrifying dream someone was about to kill you. You started running for dear life. Suddenly, you jumped up from your bed panting. With a sigh of relieve you discovered it was only a dream. It was not real. Immediately, all your sufferings disappeared. They vanished not because you killed the 'person' pursuing you in the dream but because you now know that this 'person' is not real. Whenever you suffer, you have identified your Self with the unreal, the ego. The suffering you pass through is but a 'wake up' call. The moment you wake up from your dreams (day and night) you can never suffer.

John: Lord, what is this 'way of the cross', which we must follow?

The 'Way of the Cross' is the negative path or the non-identification of the Self with the non-self (phenomena or appearances). The 'Cross' corrects your mistaken identity by tearing down all your conditioning, mental, social, and religious, plus your identification with phenomenality.

There are fourteen false identifications which are major signposts on the way of the cross.[6] The first false identity is the idea, 'I am the body'. This idea is the root of ignorance. The second is the 'name' you tag on the body and the third is the idea, 'I am male' or 'I am female'. However, the 'I am' which is your true Self is beyond the body, the name and the gender. In 'Christ', there is no male or female, black or white, Greek or Hebrew, Jew or Gentile.[7]

Those who have realized the 'I am' principle know the unity of the male and female, that is, how Eve was taken from Adam and how Adam knows itself through Eve. The two must become one in the Garden (union) of the Self.[8]

The fourth false identity is the sense of 'doership'. This is the mistaken notion that you are the one who makes things to happen. The truth is that things just happen. There is no doer separate from the deed; there is no creator separate from the created. When you think you are the doer, you assume the responsibility of the deed and thereby bind yourself to the chain (duality) of action and reaction, fate and freewill, sin and forgiveness, good and evil, and so on.

Peter: Lord, everyone has a duty in life?

Your duty is not to be this or that![9] Your duty is to be still. Be still and know that I am.[10] In 'stillness', everything is done. In 'stillness', that is, this awareness that there is nothing to become, you will align yourself to the universal 'I am'. The drop of the ego will merge with the ocean of the 'I am'. That is to say, you will not feel a separate 'I' as the doer of action but the universal I am. When you are the One in all, the concept of 'another' to whom an action can be performed cannot arise.

The fifth false identity is with geographical location. The moment you feel, 'I come from Africa', or 'I come from Israel' you bind the 'I am' to the limitations of space and time. However, space and time are mental categories. Time is nothing but the movement of thought and this movement creates space. When you arrest the flow of thoughts, you will realize the inexistence of time and space.

The sixth false identity is the veil of religion, creeds and dogmas. The statements, 'I am a Jew', 'I am a Hindu', 'I am a traditional worshiper' or 'I am an atheist' comes from the basic ignorance of the 'I am' principle. When you enquire into this 'I am' which is common in all the religions, (including the religion of those who do not believe in any religion) you will know that the 'I am' is beyond belief and unbelief.

All religions have equal validity to the truth of the 'I am'. For example, 'Yahweh' is not only for the Jews.[11] 'Yahweh', 'Christ', 'Krishna', and the 'Buddha', are one and the same 'I am' principle resident in the heart of all. All are the embodiment of God.

The seventh false identification is with language (talking). Humans have distinguished themselves from other species by the use of words. However, this ability can become an obstacle in Self-awareness when it blocks you from silence, which is the true language of the Self. Your creative Self-expression is then limited to the categories of the mind and the use of the tongue. Beyond words, silence speaks in the language of the heart. In stillness, you are one with the Self in all and you are (aware of) the resound of the primal sound in the heart of all.[12]

Learn to speak from your heart. It is the language of silence (Oneness, Love, or Consciousness). The whole of creation speaks in the language of silence and the language of silence is understood only by those who are silent. Listen to the sun, the moon, the sky, the trees, the soil…. Everything is a resound of silence.

The eighth false identity is the idea of 'me' and 'mine' or the concept of 'ownership' which ties you to properties. Ownership is the objectification of the Self. Do not feel, 'I am the creator' or 'I am the created'. Your true essence is beyond the creator, the created and its recreation. You are the One beyond conception.

The Self is everything you want. The 'I am' is your true property.

Your essence is 'wealth' unlimited by wealth, 'health' which is not determined by health and 'joy' unbounded by its own bliss.

The ninth false identity is the pride of scholarship. The truth is that the knowledge of the Self is hidden from the learned as you cannot find the Self in books.[13] Scholarship is only helpful when it leads you to humility and humility is that state where there is no trace of ego. The ego ('I' concept) is the root of all concepts, thinking, ideologies, philosophies and so on. Without the 'I' concept, there is no conceptualization. Without concepts, there is no knowledge. The Self is that which is beyond knowledge and is known by those who know that they do not know.[14]

The tenth false identity is the veil of thought. Thinking is not your true nature. Identification with thoughts prevents the awareness of the Self. When you watch your thoughts you will know that 'consciousness' which is beyond thought.

The eleventh, twelfth and thirteenth false identifications are the three states of the mind - the waking state, the dreaming state, and the deep sleep state. These three states correspond to the waking mind (conscious mind), the dreaming mind (subconscious mind) and the deep sleep mind (unconscious mind). Each state is an identification covering a more subtle one beyond it.

The day dream ('waking' state) is contradicted by the night dream (dreaming state) and vise versa. Both dreams are real as long as they last. You will never realize you are dreaming (day or night) until you wake up from the dream. When you wake up to the day dream, the night dream disappears and when you wake up to the night dream, the day dream disappears. Again, in deep sleep state, both dreams (day and night) are contradicted.

Sleep is the cause of dream as you cannot dream without being asleep. In truth, you are always asleep and as such, you are always dreaming (day or night). What you call "waking up" is actually "moving from one sleep to another" that is, from day dream to night dream and vice versa). In the night, you dream with your astral body while the physical body is sleeping (that is resting). Here you are 'dead' to the physical world. During the day, you dream with your physical body while your astral body is sleeping. Then, you are 'dead' to the astral world. It is like moving from one vehicle (astral) to another (physical). The 'night' of the astral world is the 'day' of the physical world and vice versa. The mind is responsible for this sleep, the dreams and the 'waking up' (movement) from one state to another. As long as the mind is there, the dream goes on.

The Self is beyond these three states of the mind. When the three mental states (fragmented mind) are negated, one realizes the unity of consciousness (unitary vision) and the three states, waking, dreaming and sleeping, which relates to the three worlds, gross (physical), subtle (astral) and causal (spiritual), and to the three categories of time, past, present and future, will be unified into one. Silence defragments the mind (that is, makes the mind whole or one). Silence is the only power that can wake the sleeper. This is the meaning of the scripture which says:

"Awake, O sleeper,
Rise up from the dead,
And Christ will give you light."[15]

When the sleeper awakes, he is absolute consciousness.

The final (fourteenth) false identification is with the 'I' concept. The negation of the 'I' (I am not I) is the negation of the negater. Although it is the last negation, it is actually the first and only negation because when it is negated, everything is negated and without its negation, nothing is negated.

Every object (Phenomena) has come from the 'I' subject. When the ego is stripped of all objectification, it stands naked on the Cross of Silence.[16] Naked, but unaware of its nakedness, the 'I' abides in the 'I am' as 'I am that'. 'That' awareness is the 'resurrection'.[17] Hence, without the 'Cross', there is no resurrection since the 'Christ' is the 'I-less I am'.

Epilogue:
The Resurrection

And Jesus said to Martha:
"I am the Resurrection.
Anyone who believes in me,
even though that person dies, will live,
and whoever lives and believes in me
will never die."
John 11:25

Before the beginning, there is nothing
In the beginning, there is nothing
After the beginning, there is nothing

21
The Empty Tomb
...Back to Where We Were

"In the beginning... there was formless void."
Genesis 1:1, 2

When they reached the grave
They met an empty tomb[1]
There was no one inside

If you should ever come to understand the full meaning of the 'empty tomb' as 'evidence' of the resurrection of the immortal spirit, then there is nothing else to understand.

NOTES

ACKNOWLEDGEMENTS
1 See John 4:10
2 This Book was blessed by Bhagavan Sri Sathya Sai Baba on Christmas Day, the 25th of December, 2009.

INTRODUCTION
1 The 'Father' in Christianity is the 'Yahweh' of Judaism. The 'Father' is the 'I am' principle.
2 See *Spiritan Rule of Life, Congregation of the Holy Spirit*, 101 & 8
3 The first paragraph of the *Student's Preparatory Paper* reads, *'We the students of the Spiritan International School of Theology have been trying to understand the full meaning and implications of our Spiritan calling vis-à-vis our daily formative experience. This is the Moment of Grace, and opportunity, a rare moment granted to students to take an active part in their own integral formation'.*
4 See *The Student's Preparatory Paper for the Spiritan community customary review*, (1998) by the committee set up by the governing board of the Spiritan International School of Theology, Attakwu, Enugu, Nigeria. P. 1
5 The students' preparatory paper says, *"Since this Spiritan community living is never acquired nor experienced during the initial formation, it becomes extremely difficult if not impossible to live this life later in on-going formation. 'One cannot give what one does not have.'"* See *The Students' Preparatory Paper for the Spiritan community customary review*, P. 1
6 See 'Itaici' document 1992; and the Maynooth 1998, The Congregation of the Holy Spirit, The General Chapter 1998, no 2.25, p 104.
7 Proverbs 29:15
8 John 8:32
9 In the Gospel of Mark, it is written: *"He (Jesus) used many such*

stories and illustrations to teach the people as much as they were able to understand. In fact, in his public teaching he taught only with parables, but afterward when he was alone with his Disciples, he explained the meaning to them" (Mark 4:33-34). Hence, it is evident that Jesus did not expound the high knowledge of the *'Science of the Self'* before the public because of their level of spiritual understanding. The Gospels are mainly an account of what Jesus taught in public.

10 Luke 10:21

11 Luke 8:24

12 'Nna' is an *Ibo* dialect of Eastern Nigeria.

13 Jesus once said, 'The Father and I are One' – John 10:30

14 See the works of Sri Sankaracharya, the celebrated philosopher of nondualistic Vedanta and Sri Ramana Maharshi, (1879 -1950) the naked apostle of Self Knowledge. See the classic work, *Maharshi's Gospel, The Teaching of Sri Ramana Maharshi*, (Tamilnadu: Sri Ramanasramam 2002.)

15 See the works of Rumi Jalaladin (1207-1273) especially his classics, Masnavi, and Divan-I Shams-*I Tabriz*

Chapter 1
The 'I AM' Principle

1   See Matthew 16:13-20 and Luke 9:18-21

2   John 10:34

3   Exodus 3:14

4   John 14:12 "Verily, verily I say unto you, he that believeth on me, the works that I do shall he do also"

5   Sri Ramana Maharshi, the Sage of Arunachala, told this story many times. See *Day by Day with Bhagavan*, Mudaliar A. D. (Ed.), (Tamilnadu: Sri Ramanasramam, 2002) 278. 5 Luke 12:31

6 Matthew 6:33

7   Creation is the image of God or the Self. See Genesis 1:26

8   Psalm 46:10

9   "Unless you die you will never live." – Mathew 10:39

10 Genesis 3:24

11 Desire is the 'original sin' in the Christian tradition because it is the origin of all sins.

12 Genesis 3:5

13 Eve was taken from Adam (Genesis 2:22).

14 "The woman whom you gave to be with me, she gave me of the tree and I did eat." (Genesis 3:12). This concept of Adam and Eve is similar to the Siva-Shakthi principle in the Hindu tradition. Just as Eve is the power of Adam, through Shakthi, Siva manifests itself.

15 Luke 11:9

16 John 4:10

Chapter 2
Self Knowledge

1 See John 14:5 – 9

2 According to Ramana Maharshi, 'the whole of Vedanta could be summarized into four words, *De'ham*, Am I this body; *Na'hma*, I am not; *ko'ham*, who am I?; *So'ham*, I am that. See, *Day by Day with Bhagavan*, Mudaliar A. D. (Ed.), (Tamilnadu: Sri Ramanasramam. 2002) 113.

3 Matthew 7:13

4 See The First Sermons of Buddha at Banares.

5 Luke 17:20 - 21

6 John 1:1 –The verse, 'And the Word was God' means that 'Sound' (or Word) and 'Silence' (or God) are one.

Chapter 3
The Self Alone Is

1 Mark 12:28-31, Matthew 24:34-40, and Deuteronomy 6:4-5

2 (Author's paraphrase)

3 The law (tōrāh) or Command (Micwāh) sometimes mean the whole of the Old Testament Scriptures (see John 10:34; John 12:34; *John John 15:25*). The law is also referred to as "the Ten Words" (the Decalogue, see Exodus 34:28, Deuteronomy 4:13, 10:4) or simply as "the Word" spoken by Yahweh. In Hinduism, Aum (pronounced

'OM') - which is the Creative Word of God - is the essence of the entire Vedas and if the whole of the Vedas were to be lost, it can be recovered with the single Word, 'OM'. In Islam, the whole of the Quran is regarded as the "Word of Allah" and is coded in the verse, *"La ilaha illah allah"* (God alone is). The Prophet said that this single verse (Qur'an 37:4) is the soul of Allah's revelations in the Holy Quran.

4   See Luke 11:46&52. See also Hosea 4:6 – "My people perish for want of (Self) Knowledge since you yourself (the priests) have rejected knowledge."

5   Matthew 5:17

6   Deuteronomy 6:4; Exodus 20:3.

7   The Hebrew word 'Yahweh' (Jehovah) is explained as equivalent to 'ehyeh, which is a short form of 'ehyeh 'ăsher 'ehyeh, translated in the King James Version w/Aphocripha as "I am that I am." "I am that I am" means "Self-existence" or "Pure existence".

8   The Unity of God is most fundamental and the heart of God's revelations to Prophet Muhammad (Peace be upon Him) in the Qur'an. This is expressed in the primary Kalimah of Islam as "God Alone is" *(La ilaha illa allah).* This beautiful phrase is the bedrock of Islam, its foundation and essence. It is regarded as the first pillar of Islam, **(the Shahada)**. The Prophet himself said that this verse alone (Qur'an 37:4) constitutes one third of the whole of the Qur'an (See Sahih Bukhari, Volume 9, Book 93, Number 469) and it is the expression of this belief which differentiates a true Muslim from a kafir (non-believer).

In the East, Advaita, the philosophy of oneness is the soul of Hinduism.

9   Exodus 20:4. Islam also forbids the making of images of Allah for the same reasons. If God is One and Only, where is the second to compare with Him? (Surah 112).

10 John 4:24

11 Deuteronomy 6:4

12 Acts 17:28

13 John 15:5

14 *Summer Showers in Brindavan*, (Prashanthi Niliyam: Sathya Sai Books and Publications Trust, 1974), 166. ('I am the Seed of all Being' is the basis of Indian Philosophy of Advaita.)

15 Psalm 81:9

16 In Islam, to think that there is something apart from Allah is the mark of an unbeliever who joins 'gods to God' (Qur'an 3:57).

Chapter 4
Beyond Images

3 Exodus 20:4; Deuteronomy 5:8

4 Deuteronomy 5:8

5 In most religions, we have these three fold levels of spiritual Awareness. In Christianity, Jesus initially said, *'I am the Servant of God'*. Later He affirmed *'I am the Son of God'* and finally He declared *'I and the Father are One'*. In *Zoroastrianism*, it is said: *'I am in the Light'*, *'The Light is in Me'* and *'I am the Light'*. In Hinduism, these three correspond to the *Dvaita, (Dualism), Vishistadvaita (Qualified Non-Dualism)* and *Advaita (Non-Dualism)*. While the *Vedas* deal with *Dualism*, the *Upanishads* preach *Qualified Non-Dualism* based on the concept of Unity in Diversity and *Vedanta* spells out the principle of *Advaita*.

6 Mark 14:36

7 John 11:4

8 John 10:30

Chapter 5
You are the 'I am'

1 'When you did it to one of the least of these my brothers and sisters, you were doing it to me!' – New Living Translation 2 John 8:3-11

3 Exodus 20:7, Deuteronomy 5:11

4 Deuteronomy 5:11

5 Job 1:6

6   Luke 6:31

7   Matthew 5:22

8   Leviticus 19:18, Luke 10:27

Chapter 6
The Essence of the Sabbath 1 Luke 6:6-10

2   Exodus 20:8, 11

3   In the Hindu tradition, there are seven subtle psychic energy centres called chakras or points of concentration of energy, linking the gross body to the vital force in the astral and causal bodies. The *Kundalini shakthi* or the latent divine energy is coiled at the base chakra. Its upward flow to the Crown chakra (the seventh chakra) through the intermediary centres takes one to various levels of consciousness and spiritual awakening.

4   Numbers 21:9 – While in the desert, as the people of Israel moved from the *'land'* of duality or bondage (*'I am this or that'*) to the promised *'land'* of liberation or Oneness (*'I am that I am'*) God instructed Moses to fashion a bronze serpent and raise it on a standard (rod) as a symbol of healing and wellbeing. Jesus referred to this episodes when he said, 'As Moses lifted up the bronze snake on a pole in the wilderness, so I, the Son of Man, must be lifted up on a pole, so that everyone who believes in me will have eternal life' (John 3:14-15). In the Hindu tradition, this is the awakening of the *Kundalini shakthi* or the *'Serpent Power'*.

5   Revelations 8:1

6   Revelation 11:15

7   Exodus 32:19

8   Exodus 34:1

9   'I have come not to abolish the laws, but to perfect them.' - Matthew 5:17

10 John 13:34 - the New Law is the 'I am' Love or Christ Love

11 Isaiah 11:9 *"They shall not hurt nor destroy in all my holy mountain: for the earth shall be full of the knowledge of the LORD, as the waters cover the sea."*

12 See Jeremiah 31:33-34, *"There will be no further need for anyone to teach another saying, 'Learn to know Yahweh.' No, they will all know me, from the least to the greatest."*

13 The Golden Rule, *"Treat others as you would like them to treat you"* is derived from the law of love, "The Self alone is." See Matthew 7:12. You can only treat others as your Self when you realize that the Self in you is the same Self in all.

14 Mathew 7:12. "The Self is one, be alike to everyone" is the sum of the law and the prophets.

Part IV: The Negation of the Opposites

1 The negation of the opposites is the transcendence of duality (male and female, life and death, good and bad) and the realization of the one without a second.

Chapter 7
Your True Self

1 This is the immutable law of duality.

2 See Matthew 17:1-9

3 See Matthew 17:9 and John 10:18

4 Malachi 4:5

5 Prophet Elijah lived 850 before Christ. The Jewish popular belief is that Elijah would come before the Christ. For example, in the book of Malachi, it is written, 'Behold I will send you Elijah the Prophet before the coming of the great day of the Lord' (Malachi 4:5).

6 Matthew 11:14 and 17:12

7 John 1:21

8 Matthew 6: 33

9 37 – 4 BC. This is not Herod Antipas, (4 BC – AD 39) Roman Tetrarch of Galilee who beheaded John.

10 Luke 1:5 -13

11 Matthew 11:18

12 John 1:29

13 John 1:29

14 Herod Antipas (20 BC – 39 AD) who ruled over Galilee and Pasea.

15 Mark 6:18

16 Leviticus 18:16

17   around AD 30 or 31

18 Luke 7:18

19 Mark 6:24

20 Exodus 21:1-23

21 Deuteronomy 7:3-5

22 Baal (bā´al) is the title for the supreme God among the Canaanites and the Babylonian 'Belu' or 'Bel' which means "Lord". The Babylonian Bel-Merodach was a Sun-god, and so too was the Can Baal whose full title was Baal-Shemaim, "Lord of Heaven."

23 1 Kings 18:24

24 I King 18:27

25 1 Kings 18:38

26 1 King 18:40

27 See 1 King 18:24

28 1 Kings 19:2

29 Matthew 26:52

30 Genesis 9:6

31 Galatians 6:7

Chapter 8
Beyond Good and Evil

1   See John 9:1-7

2   John 9:3

3   See Matthew 11:28 "Come to me, all you who labor and are overburdened, and I will give you rest."

4   Galatians 2:20

5   Acts 17:28

6   Matthew 25:40

7   Maharshi's Gospel, *The teachings of Sri Ramana Maharshi,*
(Tiruvamalai, Sri Ramanasramam, 2002), 30.

Chapter 9
Eternal Life

1   Matthew 16:21
2   Matthew 16:22 Peter's sorrow was like Arjuna's despondency
before the battle at Kurukshetra as narrated in the epic mystical
poem of the Hindu religion, the Bhagavad Gita, or "Song of
God". The life of Lord Krishna, the key figure in the Gita and His
closest disciple, Arjuna, was a mirror of the life of Jesus and his
head disciple, Peter. The Gita was the instruction of Lord Krishna
(2000BC) to Arjuna during the Mahabharatha war. It was a battle
between the forces of good and evil fought out at Kurukshetra
(which refers to the inner battle between the false self (the ego) and
the true Self (the I Am).

In this war, Ajurna became despondent when he saw his
uncles, grandfathers, teachers, maternal uncles, brothers, sons and
grandsons, father-in-laws, grandsons, brother-in-laws and kinsmen
stationed on the opposing side. He was possessed by extreme
compassion and said to Krishna he did not see any good slaying
his kith and kin in battle, not for the sake of any kingdom. In the
same manner, Peter, filled with compassion, tried to prevent Jesus
from death on the cross, not for the sake of any Kingdom.

Symbolically, both Peter and Arjuna could not face the war of
Self-emancipation because of their identification with the world of
phenomena. Lord Krishna's message to Arjuna and that of Lord
Jesus to Peter was the same, namely, the need for renunciation or
dispassion (yoga of detachment) in the science of Self-realization.

Jesus said to Peter, "Anyone who comes to me without hating
(that is, non identification with) father, mother, wife, children,
brothers, sisters, yes and his own life too, cannot by my disciple. If
any of you wants to be my disciple, you must renounce yourself,

take up your cross and follow me." (Luke 14:26-27)

Krishna said to Arjuna, "He by whom the world is not agitated, and who cannot be agitated by the world; he who has no expectations, who neither rejoices not hates, neither grieves not desires, who has renounced good and evil, he who is the same to friend and foe, in honor and dishonor, in cold and heat, in pleasure and pain, in praise and censure and is free from attachment, he my devotee is dear to me." (Gita, 12:15-19)

3   Jack Hawley, *The Bhagavad Gita: A Walkthrough for Westerners*, (California: New World, 2002) 13.

4   In the Christian Tradition, 'Satan' is 'the deceiver', (Revelations 12:9); 'the temper', (Matthew 4:5; 1Thesolonians 3:5); the cause of pain, sorrow, and death (John 8:44); Satan is the counterpart of the concept of *'Maya'* – (illusion) in the Hindu tradition.

5   Light – Sound - Matter or Reflection – Resound – Reaction.

6   John 15:11

7   Dislikes are negative attachments. You are negatively attached to what you renounce.

Chapter 10
Beyond the Senses

1   See John 13:4-10

2   The term, 'One another' really means, 'One and no other'.

3   Matthew 25:40 - Service to man is service to God.

4   For an exposition of *'karma yoga'* see, Prabhavananda & Isherwood C., Bhagavad-Gita, Song of God, (Chennai: Sri Ramakrishna Math, 2008), 99-109.

The other parts of this commandment, *'Loving God with the whole heart'* and *'Loving God with the entire mind'* represent in the Hindu religion the paths of *'Bakthi Yoga' and 'Jnana Yoga'* as expounded also in the Bhagavad-Gita.

5   1 Kings 18:38

6   John 6:35

7   John 7:38

8 1 Corinthians 6:19

9 This is equivalent to the Hindu food offering: *'Brahmarpanam Brahma Havir Brahmagnau Brahmanahutam Brahmaiva Thena Ganthavyam Brahma Karma Samadhina. Aham Vaishvanaro Bhutva Praninam Dehamasritah Pranapana Samayuktah Pachamyannam Chaturvidham.'*

10 *Sathya Sai Speaks*, Vol. 14 (Prashanthi Niliyam: Sri Sathya Sai Baba Publication Trust, 1999), 195.

11 In the Hindu classification of food, these correspond to the Satwic, Rajastic and *Tamastic* foods.

Chapter 11
Self Service

1 See Matthew 25:31-43

2 See Matthew 7:22-27 3 Luke 17:10

4 Matthew 6:2

5 John 6:63

6 Matthew 26:52 & Genesis 9:6

7 Luke 6:31

8 In Hinduism, there are four types of *Karmas* (actions). 1) *Karma-atheetha*, beyond *karma*, unaffected by *karma*; (2) *Nishkama Karma*, *Karma* without any desire for the fruit thereof, karma unaffected by any craving for the result there from; (3) *Sakaama* Karma, Karma with the ambition to reap and enjoy its fruit, and (4) *Karmabhrashta*, karma that knows no restraint or control.

9 Matthew 15:14

10 Psalm 89:15

11 This is called 'Satsang' in the Vedic tradition.

12 Genesis 2:24

13 John 4:14

14 This is the sin against the Self or the Holy Spirit. It is the root of all sins. See Matthew 12:31-32.

Chapter 12
Remembering God

1   See Luke 10:38-42

2   This is 'union with God through the path of devotion' or 'Bhakthi Yoga' in the Hindu Tradition.

3   John 1:3

4   Philippians 2:10

5   The word 'So-ham' is a Sanskrit word meaning 'He (is) I'.

6   The constant remembrance of God's Name *(Namasmarana)* is the Power of Hanuman in the epic story of Lord Rama as narrated in the Holy *Ramanaya* of the Hindu Religion. Hanuman unified His Consciousness with the Name of Rama that every hair in His body vibrated with the Sound of "Ram".

In Islam also, the remembrance of God, *Dhikr*, is the goal of *Salah* (or prayer) which is the second pillar of Islam. The Holy Qur'an has so many verses that illustrate the importance of *Dhikr* - "My Devotees are those who remember their Lord while standing, sitting and lying on their sides"(Qur'an, 3:191). "For those who believe, and whose hearts find Rest in the remembrance of Allah, for without doubt in the remembrance of Allah do hearts find Rest." (Qur'an, 13:27-28)

7   Psalm 127:2

8   Sai Baba says that the Atmic (I am) principle is that which is conscious between the waking and sleeping states. See *Summer Course in Brindavan, (Discourse of Sathya Baba delivered on 29-5-1990)*. The Buddha also talked about the *knowledge of the middle path*, which gives vision and knowledge and leads to enlightenment *(Nirvana)*. See The First Sermons of Buddha at Banares.

Chapter 13
Watch Your Thoughts

1   See Luke 8: 22-25, Mark 4:35-39.

2   Luke 17:3

3   The convertibility of matter and thought has been proved

by Einstein's Law of Relativity or the Equivalence of Mass and Energy. See, Albert Einstein, *Relativity: The Special and the General Theory*, Robert W. Lawson (Ed.) (Routledge: 1920) 48. In the equation, $E = mc^2$, *E* stands for *energy*, *m* stands for *mass*, and c^2 stands for a constant which is the speed of light squared. In this case, *E* will represent the *energy of thought* and mc^2 is the concrete materialization of your thought. This means that if you want to convert a particular mass into energy, you have to make the mass vibrate at the square of the speed of light. In addition, if you want to convert energy into mass, the equation will change to: $E/c^2 = m$. For the instantaneous materialization of thought energy, you have to reduce (or divide) the vibration of thought energy by the speed of light squared. This art of reduction of thought is called concentration or thought focusing.

4   Sathya Sai Speaks, (2001), Volume 22, Sri Sathya Sai Baba Publication Trust, Prashanthi Nilayam, India, P. 148

5   John 1:14

6   The body of Prophet Elijah was said to be taken away in a chariot of fire like a whirlwind (2King 2:11). There are other incidences in the scripture, which allude to this phenomenon. Enoch was said to have walked away in the Light at the end of his bodily existence. According to the Scriptures, 'he suddenly disappeared into the Light of God' (Genesis 5:24). The episode of the transfiguration is another example (Matthew 17:2). Many saints have the power of appearing suddenly in a closed room. One could understand this in the light of the convertibility of matter and thought since walls are no barriers to thought. Here, the body is instantaneously transformed into thought and again into matter.

7   Silence is the double negation of objects (thing-ness) and void (no thing-ness).

8   Genesis 1:3

9   In the spectrum of physical energy, you have visible light waves, radio waves, X rays, Gamma Rays, infrared radiations, ultraviolet radiations, etc. There are certain things you cannot do

using the visible light waves. For example, if you want to examine the skeleton of a body you have to use X rays. In the same way, when you want to chat with a friend at the other end of the globe, you have to employ the help of radio waves.

Chapter 14
The Pathless Path

1   *'Loving God with the entire Soul'* corresponds to the Hindu path of *'Jnana Yoga'* as expounded in the Bhagavad-Gita.

2   Luke 11:1

3   See Matthew 6:7-13

4   The "Prayer of Silence" is the secret prayer. See Matthew 6:6 - Jesus said to his disciples, when you want to pray, go away by your Self (that is, abide in the Self as I am I) shut the door behind you (that is, the door of the body and mind complex) and pray to your Father (that is, the 'I am') in secret.

5   Luke 18:1 & 21:36

6   *John 4:24*

7   1 Corinthians 2:11

8   *Sathya Sai Speaks*, Vol. 32 Part 1, (Prashanthi Niliyam: Sri Sathya Sai Baba Publication Trust, 2001) 178.

9   John 4:8

10   John 4:7

11   This story was told of Saint Augustine of Hippo (354-430) who was troubled by this problem - how can the mind know God? One day he was having a walk along the shores of the ocean lost in silent contemplation. As he walked, he met a little boy who had made a very small hole beside the sands of the shore and was transferring the waters of the ocean into the little hole.

Augustine was puzzled when he saw this child. He stopped and asked the little child what he wanted to do. The boy told him that he wanted to transfer the ocean into the hole he had made. The saint was amused by the child's audacity. He told the child that it was a mere waste of time.

First the hole was not big enough to contain the waters of the ocean and secondly, even if it were as big, it would take the child uncountable lifetimes to transfer the waters with the little cup in his hand. The child then raised his head and said to the saint: "So also it is for the mind to understand God!" Immediately the child disappeared and Augustine realized it was Jesus who had come as a little child to teach him this lesson.

12 The Sufi mystic, Rumi Jalaladim, used to tell his disciples, 'If you do not want to undress, do not enter the stream of truth'.

13 The statement, *'I think, therefore I am'* was at the core of the philosophy of Rene Descartes, the French Philosopher, who was later regarded as the 'father of modern Western philosophy'.

Chapter 15
Be Still and Know

1 See Luke 18:18-27

2 Luke 18:25

3 See Matthew 19:27

4 In the Vedas, the Self or Atma is described in similar terms.

5 See Matthew 6:24. The statement, 'You cannot serve both God and wealth' means that you cannot identify the Self with objects (*'I am this or that'*) and at the same time be aware of your true Self (*'I am that I am'*). Self-objectification and Self-awareness are self-contradictory.

6 Mark 4:11

7 See Luke 8:9, Mark 4:12

6 Ramana Maharshi, the sage of Arunachala, expounded this method of Self-enquiry. See, *Self-Enquiry (Vichara Sangraham) of Sri Ramana Maharshi, Mahadevan* T. M. P. (Ed.), (Tamilnadu: Sri Ramanasramam 2003).

Chapter 16
Before Time Began

1 John 8:31, 51

2   John 8:56

3   John 8:58

4   *'Eko 'ham bahuh syām' - I am One; let me be many – is at the core of Vedanta philosophy.* See, *Summer Showers in Brindavan*, (Prashanthi Niliyam: Sri Sathya Sai Baba Publication Trust, 1979), 9.

5   1 John 1:5

6   Ecclesiastes 4:8. The Qur'an has the same message: "In the Name of God, the Merciful, the Compassionate. Say He is Allah, the One and Only, Allah, the Eternal, He begetteth not, and He is not begotten; And there is none like unto Him." (Qur'an 112). The whole of the Hindu Vedanta is replete with similar sayings: "God is One, there is no second" (*Ekam Eva Adwithiyam Brahma*) and "There is only just One; those who have seen the truth praise it in many ways" (*Ekam Sath vipraah bahudhaa vadanthi*).

Chapter 17
The Universe is My Body

1   See John 6:1-15 and Matthew 14:13-21 and 15:32-38.

2   See John 6:16, 22, 25-27

3   John 6:51,

4   John 6:53,55-56

5   John 6:66

6   See Mark 14:22-24 and Luke 26:26-28.

7   Kasturi, N., *Sathyam Sivam Sundaram* Part IV, (Prashanthi Niliyam: Sri Sathya Sai Baba Publication Trust, 2003),101

8   Colossians 3:15; 1 Corinthians 10:17; 12:12-27; Romans 12:5; Ephesians 2:16; 4:4.

9   John 6:35&53

10 The prayer of St Francis of Assisi

11 The Sun contains 99% of the total mass of the solar system. In other words, if you put the planets in the solar system together, Jupiter, Saturn, Uranus, and the rest, their total mass is not up to 1% the mass of the sun.

12 A galaxy is a congregation of billions of stars held together by

gravity. The Milky Way galaxy which contains the sun is about 100,000 light years in diameter containing at least 200 billion stars. One light year is the distance a beam of light travels in one year. This is approximately six trillion miles. Venkataraman, G., (2007) *In quest of infinity*, Prashanthi Niliyam, available from: http://media. radiosai.org/Journals/Vol_05/01JAN07/04-musings.htm (assessed 28 May, 2009)

13 In the *Vedic* account of creation, *the Bhuthakasa* (Gross physical universe) is a tiny dot within the *Chittakasa* (Subtle mental space) which itself is an atom within the *Chidakasa*.(The Causal Form of the universe). Divinity is beyond and contains all these three. See *Bhagavad Gita Part 1, Divine Discourses of Sri Sai Baba*, (Prashanthi Niliyam: Sri Sathya Sai Baba Publication Trust, 2005), 19.

14 See Matthew 6:25-33

15 Luke 12:31 – "Set your hearts on God's Kingdom (that is on 'Self Knowledge'), and all these other things will be given you as well." See also verse 32: "There is no need to worry (be afraid) since it has pleased the Father (that is the 'I am') to give you the Kingdom (that is the 'I am')." In other words, there is no need to worry since you are already that, the 'I am'.

16 Mathew 6:22

17 Proverbs 15:3

18 Psalm 139; 7-12; 15.(Author's Paraphrase. Yahweh has been translated here as "the 'I am'".)

19 Ecclesiastes 1:9

20 Romans 8:22

21 1Kings 8:9; 2Chronicles 5:10

22 Acts, 17:18

Chapter 18
God from God

1 See John 10:22-24.

2 John10:30

3 John 10:33

4   See Psalm 82:6

5   See John 10:34,-36

6   Ecclesiastes 1:9 "That which has been is what will be, that which is done is what will be done, and there is nothing new under the sun."

7   John 1: 1 – "And the Word was God"

8   Colossians 1:8

9   John 1:1

10 John 1:2-3

11 Mandukya Upanishad,chapter1:v1

Part VI: The 'Cross'

1   The implication of this statement is, *'I am dead, therefore I am alive'* or *'I am not, therefore I am'. It is the negation of the false self or the ego. The realization of the 'Christ' Consciousness is the awareness of I-less I am.*

Chapter 19
Playing Death

1   Matthew 5:3-10

2   This is a Sufi story.

3   *Gems from Bhagavan*, Madaliar A. D. (Ed.), (Tamilnadu: Sri Ramanasramam, 2003), 16.

4   Ecclesiastes 10:2

5   John 14:27 "Peace I leave with you, my peace ('the 'I am' peace) I give unto you: not as the world gives, do I give to you. Let not your heart be troubled, neither let it be afraid."

6   John 15:11

7   Matthew 5:44, Luke 6:27

8   Matthew 19:21

9   Luke 6:29

10 Matthew 5:41

11 Luke 6:30

12 Luke 6:35

13 Luke 6:29

14 The Self is without cloths, that is, the Self is without any attachment.

15 Luke 6:37

16 Matthew 7:2

17 Luke 6:31, Matthew 7:12

18 Luke 9:48; 22:26, Mark 9:35, Matthew 23:11

19 Matthew 10:39, Luke 17:33; 9:24, Mark 8:35

20 John 15:19

Chapter 20
The Way of the Cross

1   Matthew 26:36, Luke 22:39, John 18:1

2   The Cabbala is the Tree of Knowledge or Adam Kadmon, that is, the primeval and universal man. It is 'planted' at the 'middle' of the 'Garden of Eden' and gives the knowledge of Life and death. See Genesis 2:9.

3   See Luke 14:26, Luke 9:23, Matthew 16:24

4   see Hosea 6:4 – "My people are being destroyed because they don't know me. It is all your fault, you priests, for you yourselves refuse to know me".

5   In the Jedeo-Christian tradition, 'Satan' is synonymous with 'separation from divinity' as a result of 'pride'. Originally, Satan was one with God (which means that the ego has no separate existence from the Self). 'Satan was seen as the 'son of God', 'angel of God' (Job 1:6) who was 'cast out', 'thrown out' or 'separated' from 'God' or 'heaven'. (Revelations 12:7-10) Hence, 'Satan' or 'ego' is the sense of separation. Because this 'sense of separation' is false (an illusion) 'Satan' is also seen as a 'deceiver', (Rev 12:9); 'father of lies', (John 8:44);   and 'tempter', (Matthew 4:5).

6   The Catholic tradition has the fourteen *Stations of the Cross*, which are representations of the *'sufferings' 'death' and 'resurrection'* of Jesus.

7   See Galatians 3:27-28 – "And all who have been united with

Christ in baptism have been made like him. There is no longer Jew or Gentile, slave or free, male or female — you are one in Christ Jesus."

8 Genesis 2:24

9 *Maharshi's Gospel, The teachings of Sri Ramana Maharshi*, (Tamilnadu: Sri Ramanasramam, 2002), 25

10 Psalm 46:10

11 The Jewish religion appropriated Yahweh as a person God which is exclusive to the Jewish nation. However, with time, this religious idea developed and Yahweh was seen to belong to all nations. See Isaiah 2:2, 4 – when all nations will stream to the Mountain of Yahweh and nation will not lift sword against nation.

12 This is the meaning of the Maharshi's statement, 'Silence is ever-speaking, it is the perennial flow of language'. *See Maharshi's Gospel, The teachings of Sri Ramana Maharshi*, op cit. 10.

13 See Luke 10:21

14 The Greek Philosopher, Socrates, used to say, *"the only thing I know is that I do not know."* This is often referred as the 'Socratic paradox' – *"I do not know therefore I am knowledge."* See Plato, *The Republic*, Book 1.

15 *Ephesians* 5:14

16 Jesus (which represents the ego of man) was crucified naked on the Cross. The Maharshi moved about without clothes. In the Hindu religion, we have the tradition of the naked sages. Rumi Jalal al - Din, (d. 1273) a Muslim mystic once said, *"If you are not ready to undress, do not enter the stream of truth."* In the Hebrew Bible, *Adam and Eve* 'moved' about in the Garden of eternal consciousness (paradise) naked. "Although they were both naked, neither of them felt any shame" (Genesis 2:25). In the state of oneness, they were unconscious of their nakedness. When the one alone exists, who is there to see another?

17 This is Sri Sathya Sai Baba's description of the essence of Christianity as inscribed in His *'Sarva Dharma'* emblem – "You must crucify the 'I' on the cross of Calvary to endure on you the

resurrection of the Immortal Spirit."

Chapter 21
The Empty Tomb

1   See, Matthew 28:6, John 20:2, Luke 24: 6, Mark 16:6

Bible quotations in this book have been taken from the following Bible versions:

1. New King James Version (NKJV)
2. King James Version w/Aphocripha (KJVA)
3. New Living Translation (NLT)
4. The New Jerusalem Bible (JB)
5. Amplified Bible (AMB)

BOOKS

O is a symbol of the world, of oneness and unity. In different cultures it also means the "eye," symbolizing knowledge and insight. We aim to publish books that are accessible, constructive and that challenge accepted opinion, both that of academia and the "moral majority."

Our books are available in all good English language bookstores worldwide. If you don't see the book on the shelves ask the bookstore to order it for you, quoting the ISBN number and title. Alternatively you can order online (all major online retail sites carry our titles) or contact the distributor in the relevant country, listed on the copyright page.

See our website www.o-books.net for a full list of over 500 titles, growing by 100 a year.

And tune in to myspiritradio.com for our book review radio show, hosted by June-Elleni Laine, where you can listen to the authors discussing their books.

MySpiritRadio